Jerry D. Thomas's

SHOEBOX KIDS
Bible Stories

BOOK 1

Kaab

thanks you

To: Kaal
From: AY Society
for reciting Morning Devotion
Texts.
Good Work!
March 29, 2003

Pacific Press® Publishing Association
Nampa, Idaho
Oshawa, Ontario, Canada

D1506969

Edited by Tim Lale
Designed by Dennis Ferree
Cover illustration by Kim Justinen
Inside illustrations by Mark Ford

Library of Congress Cataloging-in-Publication Data:

Thomas, Jerry D., 1959-
    Shoebox kids' Bible Stories/Jerry D. Thomas.
        p. cm.
    Contents: bk. 1. Creation to Abraham.
    ISBN: 0-8163-1823-9
    1. Bible stories—O.T. Genesis. [1. Bible stories—O.T.
Genesis. 2. Christian life.] I. Title.

BS551.3T48 2001
221.9'505—dc21

01 02 03 04 05 • 5 4 3 2 1

CONTENTS

BIBLE STORY ADVENTURES

FOR KIDS:

The Bible is full of stories from long ago. And while it's fun to learn about the people and the places, it's also important to see how what the Bible says affects the way we live today—especially if we are trying to be friends of Jesus. *Bible Story Adventures* helps you do both.

Every chapter is a double story—first, a story from the Bible, then a story from today that shows one of the lessons that Bible story can teach us. That story—with *The Shoebox Kids*—is about learning what the Bible really means—at home, at school, or on the playground.

Every story is an adventure in learning to be more like Jesus!

FOR PARENTS AND TEACHERS:

Bible Story Adventures does more than just give children information about the Bible—it shows them how to apply that information to everyday life. Teaching our children means going beyond information and entertainment to helping them learn to apply Bible truths. Too many of us grew up learning about the Bible but not getting to know God. We can help the children we love by showing them not just what the Bible says, but what difference it makes in how we live and how we love others.

Every Bible story has many lessons to teach, and each *Shoebox Kids* story can only teach one of those. There may be others you can help your child learn.

The questions at the end of each story can help you see what your child or children understand and what they may be confused about. Many of the questions can be discussion-starters that will help you understand your children better. They can help open the doors of communication, which are so important to reassuring them of your love and teaching them about God's love.

Jerry D. Thomas

MEET THE SHOEBOX KIDS!

The Shoebox Kids are six friends who go to the same church. Their Sabbath School class meets in a really small room in the church. It's so small that everyone calls it "the Shoebox." And their teacher's name is Mrs. Shue (pronounce it just like "shoe"). So everyone calls them the Shoebox Kids.

Maria and Chris Vargas are Shoebox Kids. They live with their mom and dad and their little sister, Yolanda (everyone calls her Yoyo). Maria is in the fourth grade; Chris is in the third grade. They both are in the same classroom at their small church school.

Jenny Wallace is a Shoebox Kid. Her parents are divorced, and she lives with her mother and her cat, Butterscotch. Her father lives nearby, and she spends many weekends with him. She's in the fourth grade at the local public school.

Sammy Tan is a Shoebox Kid. He lives with his grandparents and is in the fourth grade in the church school. His parents were killed in a car crash when he was very young. He has one uncle.

Willie Teller is a Shoebox Kid. He lives with his parents and his dog, Coco. Willie cannot use his legs for walking and wheels around in a cool wheelchair. He's in the fourth grade at the same public school as Jenny, but they're not in the same classroom.

DeeDee Adams is a Shoebox Kid. She lives with her parents and her older sister. She's in the third grade at the church school with Chris, Maria, and Sammy.

The Shoebox Kids live in Mill Valley, but they visit a lot of other interesting places. As they study their Bible lesson each week, they find that God is helping them learn about being His friend and treating others as Jesus did.

CHAPTER 1

IN THE VERY BEGINNING
Maria's Own World

At the very beginning of time, God created the universe. He scattered the stars and started the planets spinning.

On our planet, God's Holy Spirit moved over the deep waters. The whole world was empty like a blank piece of paper waiting to be painted. But it wasn't going to stay that way! God's week of Creation was about to begin.

To get things started, God said, "Let's have some light!" And from nowhere, light shone across the water. God saw the light and liked it. "Good," He said. "I'll call the light 'day' and the darkness 'night.'"

And that was the first day.

On the second day, God said, "We need something to divide the water—we need some above and some below." So He made the air. Some of the water stayed up above in the clouds, and the rest stayed below. God looked at the air He had created and liked it. He said, "I'll call the air 'sky.'"

On the third day, God said, "Let's move the water so we can have some dry land." So He moved the water until there was dry land in many places. Then God looked at what He had done and liked it. He said, "I'll call the dry land 'dirt', and the water will be called seas and lakes and rivers."

But God wasn't finished yet. He said, "Let's have some plants and trees growing in our dirt. We'll need grass and flowers and bushes and trees of every kind."

As He spoke, the dirt disappeared under a blanket of green grass. Bright flowers popped up out of nowhere. Suddenly, tall trees reached for the sky. Big green leaves covered the new grass with shade.

Then God said, "We need plants that grow grain for seeds and trees that grow fruit for its seeds. Every grain seed will grow into a grain plant. Every fruit seed will grow into a fruit tree."

Fields of wheat and rice spread across the land, their grains waving in the breeze. Fruit trees appeared, holding out their branches filled with apples, oranges, bananas, walnuts—tasty treats of every size and color.

"This is good," God said. And that was the end of the third day.

On the fourth day of Creation, God said, "We need lights in the sky—one for the day and one for the night." So the sun appeared in the sky. Whenever the sun was shining, it was daytime. God made the moon to help the stars light the sky at night.

So God looked at the sun and moon He had made to give the earth light. And God said, "This is good."

And the first part of the Creation week was over. God had painted His world bright and beautiful and soft and quiet.

Maria's Own World

What are we going to do tomorrow?" Maria Vargas asked as she got ready for bed. Since Christmas was over, and her new toys didn't seem so new anymore, Maria thought the next day might be boring.

"Don't you need to work on your science fair project?" Mrs. Vargas asked. "Your teacher told me that the fair was coming up soon."

"What should I do?" Maria wondered out loud. "Make a poster like I did last year?"

"Think about it before you go to sleep," her mom suggested. "But remember to read your Sabbath School lesson first."

Maria opened her lesson. "It's about God creating the world. Now that would have been a great science project!"

Mrs. Vargas laughed. "You know, that's not a bad idea."

Maria raised one eyebrow. "It is a good idea, Mom. It's just a little more homework than I wanted to do during this vacation."

"No, I mean you could make a globe. You know, a round ball painted like the world."

Maria liked that idea. "I could paint on all the mountains and rivers. And . . . wait a minute. How would I make it round?"

"We could use a balloon," Mrs. Vargas answered.

Maria nodded. "We could use a balloo . . . Mom! How could I paint on a balloon? It would pop!"

Mrs. Vargas laughed. "I'll show you tomorrow. Now finish your lesson and go to sleep."

Maria mumbled to herself as she settled down under her covers. "Paint on a balloon—why couldn't she show me tonight? What could we do—wrap the balloon with drawing paper?"

She was still mumbling about it when she went to sleep.

The next morning after breakfast, Mrs. Vargas got out her mixing bowl. "Now, Maria, I'll show you how to make a world. Mix this flour in with that water."

Maria looked at her. "Are you sure? The last time I did something like this, I got in trouble."

"Go ahead. Mix it up." Maria mixed. When Mrs. Vargas told her to stop, she washed her hands and waited for the next instructions. "Now, run to your room and get one of those red balloons we didn't use at Yoyo's birthday party."

Maria shook her head, but she ran and brought the balloon to the kitchen. Before long, she was out in the living room. "Dad, are you through with the newspaper?"

He nodded as he turned the last page. "I am now."

"Can I have it?"

Mr. Vargas smiled. "Are you looking for science project ideas?"

Maria shrugged her shoulders. "No. I just want to tear it into shreds."

"What?"

Maria laughed. "Hey, don't blame me—it was Mom's idea."

"It's called papier-mâché (pa-per ma-shay)," Mrs. Vargas said from the doorway. She held up the fat red balloon. "Now, start ripping up that paper before the paste dries."

She showed Maria how to tear the paper into skinny strips. "Put the last full newspaper pages on the table to protect it. We'll put the balloon there. Then we'll dip the strips into the flour-and-water paste."

Maria watched while she slipped one strip under the oozing sticky stuff. It came out all slimy. "Mom, that's gross."

"Just watch." She slapped the wet paper onto the red balloon. It stuck to the surface. "Now, you do it. And keep doing it until you can't see red anymore."

"OK," Maria said. She dipped another strip into the paste. "Eww, it's yucky." But as she slapped the strip against the balloon, she smiled. "I like it."

Before long, the balloon was covered. "Now, we'll wait until it dries," Mrs. Vargas said.

"I still don't think this is going to work," Maria said. "It's too mushy and much too wet to paint."

An hour later, Maria changed her mind. *Tap, tap.* "Look, Mom. It's hard!"

"Very good," Mrs. Vargas said. "Now, put on another layer of paper strips."

Maria slapped the strips on. She slapped on three more layers that afternoon. Finally, after supper, it was finished. "I'm going to paint the oceans first," Maria said as she got out the blue paint container and a map. She worked hard, and before long, gray land was surrounded by water on her world.

She was painting South America brown when her brother came in. "What is that?" he asked. "And why is it on the table?"

"It's my world," Maria said. "I made it from a balloon."

"A balloon?" Chris asked. "Let's see what happens if it pops." He reached for a fork, and Maria screamed.

"Mom! Chris is trying to pop my world."

Mrs. Vargas arrived in time to stop the disaster. "Chris, leave your sister's world alone. Maria, stop shouting. It won't hurt to pop the balloon now. When the paste dried on the paper, it formed a shell around the balloon. You can stick in a pin and let the air out if you want."

Yoyo came in as her sister was poking the world with a pin. "What is it, Maria? What did you make?"

"I made a world," Maria said.

Yoyo was puzzled. "What did you make it out of?" She tapped the gray shell. "What's inside of it?"

Maria frowned. "Well, it was a balloon, but I let the air out of that. There's nothing inside now."

Yoyo stared for a minute. When Mr. Vargas stepped in, she ran to him. "Daddy, Maria made a world out of nothing."

He raised one eyebrow and looked at Maria. "That's quite a trick."

Maria rolled her eyes. "I just made a globe of the world out of papier-mâché. Now I'm painting in all the countries and stuff." She painted the North Pole white. "This is fun. I wonder what God felt like when He created the world. I would have liked deciding where to put the rivers and lakes."

"It would be great to think up all the animals and plants to put on a new world," Chris said.

Mrs. Vargas smiled. "I think God felt a lot like you feel now. I think He likes creating beautiful things. That's one of the ways we are the most like God. We like to create things too."

"Like papier-mâché worlds," Maria agreed.

"Like forts and treehouses," Chris added.

"Like children," Mr. Vargas said with a smile.

Yoyo wanted to say something too. "Like when I make . . . a mess in my room!"

Everyone had to laugh about that. "Mom, can I take my world to the Shoebox this Sabbath?" Maria asked. "Since our lesson is about Creation, I want to show everyone the world I created—out of nothing!"

QUESTIONS

1. Do you like to make things? Then you're like God too!

2. Which part of God's created world do you like best?

3. If you could create a world, what would it look like?

4. Isn't it nice to know that the same God who created the world out of nothing is your Friend?

A PLANET FULL OF LIFE

Sammy's Favorite People

When the sun came up on the fifth day, the earth was quiet and still. Nothing was moving but the leaves on the trees.

God had painted a world of bright and beautiful colors. But He wanted more than just colors—He wanted sounds and motion. He wanted a planet full of life.

God said, "Let's fill the air and seas with amazing creatures. I want birds of every kind soaring though the air on wings and feathers. I want fish with fins and scales swimming in the seas and lakes and rivers. I want swimming mammals to join them in their watery home."

Suddenly every tree seemed to be filled with singing birds. Explosions of red, blue, and green feathers filled the skies as parrots, cardinals, and blue jays lifted their wings to fly.

Beneath the waves, schools of fish suddenly swam together like perfectly trained marching bands. Deeper down, squids and eels slipped through the dark water.

On the surface, whales and dolphins jumped up into the bright sunlight then fell with mighty splashes.

God looked at what He had created, and He was delighted. "Go out and fill the world with your children," He said to His creatures.

On the sixth day, God had one place left to fill with creatures. "I want the land to be filled with animals," He said. "Wild animals and tame animals, even the tiny bugs—and I want each one to have children and fill the land."

With those words, antelopes and horses thundered across the plains. Raccoons and monkeys scampered up trees. Elephants and sheep grazed on the fresh green grass.

And God looked at His animals and smiled. Because He knew what He had created was good.

God's wonderful creation only needed one more thing. He said, "Let's make people—human beings who are like Us. We'll put them in charge of all the creatures—birds, fish, animals, and bugs."

And so God took dust and dirt and shaped it into a human form. Carefully He shaped each bone, muscle, and organ. Then He breathed into its nostrils, and the human being came to life! That's how He made Adam, the first man who ever lived. God took Adam to a special place to live—a Garden called Eden, where every kind of tree and plant grew.

"This is your home," God told Adam. "Take care of the trees and the plants. The animals are yours also. You should give them each a name."

So God and Adam walked through the Garden as Adam learned to care for each of the plants and animals.

Each animal was as special to him as our pets are to us. God led each animal and bird to Adam, and Adam gave each one a name.

As much as Adam liked all the animals, he noticed that there were two of each of them and only one of him! He looked but he didn't see any other people.

But God had a plan. He put Adam into a deep sleep and carefully took a rib from Adam's side. The way God did it, there was no pain and no scars. Instead of using dirt and dust, He used Adam's rib to create another person—the first woman, Eve.

When Adam opened his eyes, God must have said, "I have a surprise for you." Then He led Eve to Adam.

Adam must have stared and blinked. Finally he said, "Thank you, God. Now there's someone like me—only different. Since she was made from my rib, she's already part of me."

God took their hands and blessed them and said, "The world is yours. Fill it with your children. The animals, birds, and plants are yours to use. Take care of them and of each other."

So at the end of the busy sixth day, God performed the first wedding. Then He looked at everything He had done and smiled. "This is very good." He said.

Sammy's Favorite People

This must be Abraham Lincoln!"

Sammy Tan just stood there with his hands folded and a big smile on his face.

"How did you create these little people?" Pastor Hill asked. Pastor Hill, the pastor at their church, was one of the judges for the Science and Art Fair at Sammy's school. He was looking closely at Sammy's project.

Sammy pointed to the small figures on the table. "They are Abraham Lincoln, George Washington, and Theodore Roosevelt. I carved them out of soap. Then I used shoe polish to paint their faces and clothes. In social studies, we've been learning about American history."

"And your project is about great presidents," Pastor Hill finished for him. "You did a good job, Sammy." Pastor Hill wrote on his pad of paper and went on to look at the other projects.

Sammy sighed and relaxed a little. He knew that his carved people weren't perfect. *Hey, carving soap isn't easy,* he said to himself. *And it's even harder to color the faces and clothes. But I think it's fun.*

The truth was, the only figure anyone could recognize was Abraham Lincoln—and only because of his hat. "Hey," Chris whispered from his place in front of his poster, "how did you do?"

Sammy shrugged. "I don't know. He liked the people I carved, but I think he liked Maria's globe better."

Pastor Hill and the other judges walked around in the school gym. They went from one project to the next, asking questions and making notes. Then they sat together to decide which project would win the prizes.

"OK, everyone," Mrs. Peterson said a few minutes later from the stage, "we're ready to announce the winners. I have the decision of the judges in my hands. Third prize goes to . . ."

Sammy held his breath. *It doesn't matter if I win or not,* he told himself.

"Third prize goes to Pete Wolske!" Sammy joined in the loud clapping as Pete went up to get his white ribbon. Mrs. Peterson shook Pete's hand. "Good job on your rocket model, Pete." Then she looked back at her list. "Now for second prize."

Sammy kept talking to himself. *I enjoyed making my soap people, and I'm glad I did it even if someone else wins the prizes.*

"Second prize goes to Angela Jackson!" Everyone clapped as Angela went up for her red ribbon. "Angela's collection of leaves was well done. Good work, Angela." Mrs. Peterson turned to pick up the blue ribbon. "Now for the first prize winner."

Sammy closed his eyes.

"The first prize goes to Maria Vargas and her world globe!" Sammy clapped and cheered with everyone as Maria ran to the stage. He felt a little disappointed, but not too much.

"I knew you would win," Sammy told Maria later when he was packing his soap figures back into the box. "That globe was a great idea."

"Thanks. I really like your soap people," Maria said. "Will you show me how to carve soap like that sometime?"

"Sure—if you'll show me how to do papier-mâché."

"Hey, Sammy," DeeDee called from the door. "Your grandmother and my mother are waiting in the van. They said to tell you to hurry."

For a second, Sammy was confused. "Oh, yeah. We're supposed to help at the Soup Kitchen for homeless people tonight. I'll see you later, Maria."

In the van, Sammy sat next to his grandmother. "You did very well, Sammy," she said.

"Well, I'm not that good at soap carving," Sammy admitted. "And I'm not too good at painting. But I still like my people better than anything else at the fair."

"I like them best too," Grandmother Tan said. "And I think we like them best for the same reason."

"Why?"

She smiled. "Because you made them."

Sammy smiled all the way to the kitchen. He helped stir the soup and put out the bowls as the hungry people came in. "Hey, Sammy," DeeDee whispered, "see that guy, the one who looks like a pirate? He looks mean, doesn't he?"

"He sure does," Sammy agreed, seeing his scowling face and dirty clothes. "Is he dangerous?"

DeeDee laughed. "No, he's really a nice person. He fixed a flat tire for us one night out on the street." She waved at him, and he smiled back.

Sammy watched the line of people coming in. A woman wearing at least three coats mumbled to herself. A man who looked as though he hadn't ever taken a bath stumbled and fell against the wall. "Do you know all of these people?" he asked DeeDee.

"Not all of them," DeeDee answered. "But a lot of them come in every week."

Sammy was amazed. "Why? I know they don't have

any place to live. I know some have lost all their money and everything. But aren't they trying? Don't they want to live in a real house again with their families?"

DeeDee shrugged. "I guess some of them don't. This is where they have lived for years."

Sammy watched the dirty man stumble up and get his bowl of soup. "Then why do you keep helping them?"

DeeDee's mom had been listening. "Because they need help, Sammy."

"But if they don't even care about helping themselves, why bother?" Sammy asked. "They'll just be here tomorrow."

Mrs. Adams shrugged. "Jesus asked us to take care of the poor and the hungry. And these people are hungry."

Sammy was still not sure. "I don't know why God keeps loving people who don't even care about themselves."

His grandmother spoke up. "Sammy, I'm surprised. You, of all people, should know that."

Sammy raised one eyebrow and shrugged.

"Even if these people have made a mess of their lives," Grandmother Tan continued, "even if they're not the best workers or fathers or mothers, God still loves them. After all, He made them."

Sammy thought about his soap people. "I see. I like my soap people best, even if they aren't perfect, because I made them. God loves all people, even if they aren't perfect, because He made them."

He looked at Mrs. Adams. "You're right. God created these people. Let's help Him take care of them." And he went to get more bowls.

<u>QUESTIONS</u>

1. Does your school have a science or art fair this year? What project will you do?

2. Have you tried soap carving? It's fun, but be sure an adult shows you how to do it safely.

3. How do you feel about things you have made? Do you like them better because you created them?

4. God loves all people, because He created us in a special way. He made us like Him!

CHAPTER

A SPECIAL DAY

Surprise! Happy Birthday!

As the sun went down at the end of the sixth day of Creation, God had a special plan for the seventh day. He was going to do something different—something He hadn't done all week.

He had already created the sun, the moon, and the stars. He had formed the world—the seas, the dry lands, and the sky. Then He filled them with trees, plants, and living creatures of every kind. Finally God created people—Adam and Eve—to love and to take care of His world.

Six times God had looked at His work and decided that it was good. Now—on the seventh day—He looked at it and decided that it was finished.

So on the seventh day God rested. Not because He was tired, but because He wanted to celebrate His creation. He blessed the seventh day and said, "This will be a holy day."

On that seventh day, God must have walked through

the Garden of Eden with Adam and Eve. They probably watched the wallabies, tiptoed past the turtles, and followed the fireflies. With every new thing that Adam and Eve saw, they thanked God again.

"It's all for you," God said. "And so is this day. Every week, this will be a Sabbath for you, a day of rest. It will be a special day when you can stop all your work and spend time with me."

So Adam and Eve spent their first Sabbath with God under the shade of the trees in the Garden of Eden.

God said, "All the fruit trees in this garden are here for you. Their fruit is yours to eat. But two trees are special." The first one was the Tree of Life. As God handed them the delicious fruit from that tree, He said, "As long as you eat the fruit from this tree, you will live forever. It is my gift to you."

Then He showed them another tree with beautiful fruit. "This is the Tree of the Knowledge of Good and Evil. If you eat this fruit, you will die."

Adam and Eve were shocked. They had never seen anything die—not even a leaf or a bug.

God explained. "You can be safe by staying away from the tree. It will be a test of your love for me."

So Sabbath is a celebration of the beautiful, perfect world God created and filled with amazing creatures of every kind. Adam and Eve could remember every week that God had done all of this for them. And that it was His plan that their perfect world would last forever.

Surprise! Happy Birthday!

This was the most boring day ever," Jenny complained. She stared out the window as the gray day turned into a black night.

"Hmm," her mother said from the couch. She was looking at Jenny's Sabbath School lesson for that week. "We could have a birthday party."

Jenny whirled around. "A birthday party? It's not my birthday. It's not your birthday. The nearest birthday to today that I know about is Willie's. And that was last week."

Her mother's eyes twinkled. "Then it will be a real surprise party!"

"Mom! It's not anyone's birthday. What are you talking about?"

"Let me explain." While her mother talked, Jenny's eyes got bigger.

"Oh," she said. "Oh! That's right! It'll be a surprise party, that's for sure. Let's call Mrs. Shue."

Sabbath morning, a light could be seen under the Shoebox door while the rest of the church was still dark. If someone were listening closely, they might have heard the sound of a table scraping across the floor or someone giggling.

Finally, it was time for church. The Vargases arrived first. Chris stopped in the hall to tie his shoe. Maria grabbed the doorknob of the Shoebox door and pushed. Nothing happened.

A SPECIAL DAY

"Hey, what's going on?" Chris asked. "Is Mrs. Shue here?"

Maria shrugged. "I don't know, but the door is locked. Do you think we should knock?"

Sammy came up while they were talking. "I wonder if Mrs. Shue is sick or gone," he said. "Maybe they cancelled our class like they close school sometimes."

"What are you guys doing out here?" DeeDee asked as she arrived. "Why don't you go in?"

"Duh, why didn't we think of that?" Chris said, smacking his forehead. "Because we can't," he told DeeDee. "The door's locked."

Willie rolled up behind everyone. "Why is the Shoebox class out in the hall today?"

"Because we can't get in!" everyone said together.

Willie reached out and turned the doorknob. The door squeaked open. "Why not?"

Everyone looked at Maria. She shrugged. "Well, it was locked before! It was! Come on, let's go in."

Willie was the first one through the door. "Wow," he whispered. There were streamers hanging from the ceiling and from the backs of the chairs. Balloons pulled at their strings from the four corners of a table at the front of the room. On that table sat a cake almost covered with burning candles. On the wall behind the cake was a big banner that said 'Happy Birthday!'"

"Welcome, everyone," Mrs. Shue called from the back. "I'm so glad you could make it to our party."

Jenny slipped out from behind the door. "Let's sing 'Happy Birthday' and blow out the candles before the whole cake catches on fire."

"But—but . . ." Maria tried to say something, but loud singing from Jenny and Mrs. Shue drowned out her voice. Finally, everyone joined in.

"Happy birthday to you, happy birthday to you . . ."

"Whose birthday is it?" Maria asked as soon as the song was over. Jenny ignored her and went over to the window.

"Now we'll blow out the candles," Jenny said. She pushed the window open, and the cold winter wind blasted in. *Whoosh!* The candles flickered, then went out. Jenny slammed the window shut and pulled the curtain closed.

"Jenny, is it your birthday?" Sammy asked.

"No, not mine," Jenny answered. "But it is one you've all celebrated before."

"It must be Mrs. Shue's birthday," Chris decided. "Happy Birthday, Mrs. Shue."

She chuckled. "Thank you, Chris, but it's not my birthday. But it is a celebration I've enjoyed over and over."

Willie snapped his fingers. "I know. It must be for Martin Luther King's birthday. We celebrated that holiday this week at school."

Mrs. Shue shook her head. "Martin Luther King Day is a special holiday. And it's a good idea to celebrate what Dr. King's work gave us—equal rights for everyone of every color. But that's not what we're celebrating."

"Is it Pastor Hill's Birthday?" DeeDee asked. "Is he coming in so we can all shout 'Surprise?'"

"No, that's not it," Jenny said. "I'll give you a clue." She went back to the window and pulled open the curtains. "Ta-da!"

A SPECIAL DAY

Everyone stared out the window. Maria tapped her foot. "Jenny, no one's there," she said. Jenny just smiled.

Chris stuck his nose on the windowpane. "I can see Mrs. Othmeyer getting out of her car in the parking lot. That was just about the right number of candles for her. Is it her birthday?"

"No, Chris." Jenny rolled her eyes. "And there wasn't enough room on the cake for all the candles that should be there."

Everyone was quiet for a minute. "I don't know anyone that old," Sammy said.

"I'll give you another hint," Mrs. Shue said. "We celebrate this birthday every week right here."

"I get it!" Willie shouted. "Sabbath! We celebrate Sabbath here every week. But how is that like a birthday, Mrs. Shue?"

"When God finished all His creation, He rested on the seventh day and called it Sabbath. He set it apart as a special time to worship Him and remember that He created us. Sabbath is the earth's birthday."

"So every Sabbath is God's way of saying, 'Let's have a party!'" Chris decided. Everyone laughed.

"I guess you're right, Chris," Mrs. Shue said. "It's a celebration, a party, an invitation to stop and remember God—no matter where we are."

Jenny's smile was the biggest of all. "So this is the earth's birthday party. Everyone gets a piece of cake. I knew we needed a good reason to have a party. I just forgot that we have one every week!"

Surprise! Happy Birthday!

QUESTIONS

1. Did you guess whose birthday it was before Willie did?

2. Did you ever think of Sabbath as a party? What are some ways we celebrate Sabbath?

3. What do you think Adam and Eve did on the first Sabbath? What would you have done?

4. Sabbath is God's invitation to you—He wants you to come to His party!

CHAPTER

GOD'S PROMISE
Danger on Runaway Ridge

Long, long ago in heaven, an angel named Lucifer decided he wasn't happy. He decided that heaven wasn't paying enough attention to him. "I'm faster, stronger, and smarter than any other angel," he said to himself. "The angels should be looking at me as much as God."

Lucifer was beginning to love himself more than he loved God. He began to think that God really didn't love him at all. He decided, "Why should I listen to what God says? I'm just as smart as God. Everyone should be listening to what I say."

God tried to talk to Lucifer. He tried to help Lucifer see that being selfish was only going to cause pain and sadness.

But Lucifer made up his mind to be God's enemy. He talked many of the other angels into joining him to fight against God. They started a war in heaven, and God had no choice—He threw them out. From then on, Lucifer was known as Satan.

When Satan heard about the people on God's new world, he began planning to get them to join him as enemies against God.

God knew that Satan would come to tempt Adam and Eve and try to get them to doubt God's love. He knew He couldn't just keep Satan away from them. Adam and Eve had to be free to choose whom to believe. But He only let Satan tempt them at one spot in the garden—the Tree of the Knowledge of Good and Evil.

Adam and Eve were safe as long as they chose to stay away from that tree. But one day, Eve wandered away from Adam. She was walking near the tree when she was surprised to hear a voice call out to her.

"Did God really say that you can't eat the fruits from any trees in this garden?"

Eve was surprised to see that a snake was talking to her from the branches of the tree. She knew that snakes were very clever creatures, but she didn't expect one to talk to her. Of course, it was Satan speaking to her through the snake.

Eve answered, "God said that we could eat fruit from all the trees except this one. He said that if we just touched the fruit of this tree, we would die!"

"That's not true," the snake said. "God knows that if you eat this fruit, you'll know everything, just like He does." Then the snake dropped a fruit into Eve's hand. "See, you touched it and you didn't die."

Eve looked at the fruit. It looked beautiful and delicious. And she liked the idea of being as smart as God.

So she took a bite. Then she ran to share her fruit with Adam.

When Adam saw what Eve had done, he was sad. But he didn't want to lose Eve. He decided that if she was going to do something wrong, he would too. He took a bite of the fruit.

Adam and Eve had always worn robes of light. Now those clothes made of light faded away, and they realized that they were naked. When God came to walk with them that evening, they ran away and hid from Him.

"Adam?" God called. "Eve? Where are you?"

Finally they answered. "We're hiding because we don't have any clothes."

God must have shaken His head sadly. "Why did you eat the fruit when I told you not to?"

Adam pointed to Eve. "She gave me some of the fruit, so I ate it."

Eve pointed toward the tree. "The snake tricked me."

God knew the truth. Adam and Eve had decided to trust Satan's words instead of God's. He said, "From now on, snakes will crawl through the dust, and people will treat them like enemies." But God knew that it was Satan who had tricked Eve. He spoke to Satan. "One day, one of Eve's children will destroy you."

God must have had tears in His eyes by now. He told Adam and Eve, "You must leave your garden. You cannot eat fruit from the Tree of Life anymore. From now on, you will have to work hard and sweat to grow your food. Now there will be weeds and thorns and pain and death. You will not die today, but when you do, your body will turn back into the dust it was created from."

So Adam and Eve left the Garden of Eden to find a new home. Angels guarded the gates to the Garden with bright, shining swords so that no one could go back inside .

Adam and Eve were very, very sad when they saw the first leaves begin to turn brown and die. They must have cried every time they saw a hurt bird or a dead animal. But God comforted them by giving them a promise. Someday, Someone was coming who would destroy Satan and sin. Someday, they would get to go back to their Garden. Jesus was coming and He would make the whole world a new Garden of Eden.

Danger on Runaway Ridge

Can we go? Can we? Can we?"

Mr. Vargas put his hands over his ears. "Chris, I heard you. Now stop asking long enough for me to think."

Chris looked at his sister, Maria, and crossed his fingers. She nodded. They really wanted to go sledding, and Chris's friend Ryan had invited them to go with his family.

Finally, Mr. Vargas spoke. "Well, I guess you can go. But, but . . ." he waited for the cheering to stop, "but you must obey Ryan's mom, and you can only sled on Pioneer Hill."

"Thanks, Dad," Maria called as she ran to find her gloves and boots.

"Dad, I wanted to try sledding down Runaway Ridge

this year," Chris said. "Everyone says it's the best sled ride in town."

"It's also dangerous," Mr. Vargas reminded Chris. "But I'll tell you what. I have to go in to town for a while this afternoon. I'll stop on my back, and we'll take a ride down Runaway Ridge together."

"Great!" Chris shouted. "Promise?"

Mr. Vargas laughed. "I promise. But you promise to stay off of it until I get there."

Every time it snowed, Pioneer Park was crowded with sleds and people. Pioneer Hill was the perfect sledding hill. It started off steep, but leveled out so that you could slide a long way and slow to a stop.

"I'm going down Runaway Ridge when my dad gets here," Chris told Ryan on their first trip to the top. They both turned to look down the backside of the park hill. Several teenagers were shouting as they flew down the slope called Runaway Ridge.

"It does look fast," Ryan said. "But so does Pioneer Hill. Come on, I'll race you to the bottom."

They both jumped on their sleds and skimmed over the snow. "Look out!" Ryan called as he almost crashed into Chris.

"See you at the bottom," Chris called as he pulled ahead. *My sled is faster than anyone's,* he thought as he slowed to a stop. *I'm probably going almost as fast as those kids on Runaway Ridge.*

Chris, Ryan, and Maria went up and down the hill for more than an hour. Finally, Ryan's mom said, "Just a few more minutes."

GOD'S PROMISE

Chris looked around for his dad. *I should have known he wouldn't really come,* Chris thought. *And he promised!* He walked slowly up the hill. By the time he reached the top, Ryan and Maria were already on their way to the bottom.

"Hey, watch this," someone shouted behind him. A teenager was trying to go down Runaway Ridge standing up on his sled. He hadn't gone far before he fell in a snow bank and bounced up laughing.

I could go down Runaway Ridge. I could do it alone, Chris thought. *I know I promised not to, but no one will ever know. Dad isn't coming like he promised he would.*

Chris took one look over his shoulder to be sure no one saw him. Then he headed for the jump-off spot on Runaway Ridge. Suddenly, it seemed very quiet. *Where did everyone go?* Chris wondered as he looked around. Even the teenagers were gone. *Good*, he thought, *no one will see me.*

OK, he thought as he bent down over his sled, *all I have to do is steer to the right of those trees and away from that ditch.* He took a deep breath and jumped.

Whoosh! The snow flew by underneath Chris's sled. *Wow, I'm really moving now!*

The sled hit a bump. "Woof!" Chris held on as the sled left the ground. "Whoa! I'm going too fast! Help!"

When he hit the next bump, Chris flew one direction and his sled flew in another. As he hit the ground, Chris saw the sled slipping past. He saw a tree headed right for him. Then there was a crash and for a few minutes he didn't see anything at all.

"Oooh," Chris moaned as he woke up. He tried to move. "Ouch, my arm hurts. And I'm freezing. Where am I?" He pushed the tree limb away with his other arm and looked around. Then he remembered.

"I'm somewhere on Runaway Ridge. I crashed, and no one knows I'm here. Oh, boy, am I in trouble."

Chris tried to see through the tree limbs to the top of the hill, but he couldn't. He started shivering. "Help! Help!" he shouted. "I'm s-stuck under a tree! Help!"

There was no answer. In fact, Chris could hear nothing at all. All he knew was, his arm hurt, his head hurt, he couldn't get up, and he was alone. "God, p-please help me," he prayed out loud. "Please s-send s-someone to find me."

It started to snow again as Chris closed his eyes. *I wonder if Maria or Ryan has noticed that I'm missing,* he thought. *I wonder why I broke my promise.*

A gust of wind brought a clump of snow down on Chris's head. It also brought a sound to his ears.

What was that? he wondered. "Hey! Help! Help, I'm over here!" He shook the tree branch he could reach. "Help!"

"Chris? Chris, is that you?"

It was the best sound Chris had ever heard. "Dad! I'm over here!"

Later that night, the family was gathered around Chris's bed. Chris's right arm was in a cast, and there was a bandage on his head. "How are you feeling, honey?" his mom asked.

"I'm fine now," he answered. "Dad, I sure am sorry I broke my promise. And I'm sure glad you kept yours."

GOD'S PROMISE

Mr. Vargas patted Chris's leg. "I'm glad you weren't hurt any worse. I know God helped me find you. And I know I don't have to tell you why it's important to keep your promises."

That week at the Shoebox, the lesson was about God's promise to Adam and Eve when they sinned. "Even though they had disobeyed God, He still loved them like a father loves his children. He promised to save them. He promised that someday, Jesus would come. And Jesus did."

Chris knew just how Adam and Eve must have felt.

QUESTIONS

1. Have you ever been snow sledding? Did you like it?

2. Have you ever made a promise and not kept it? How did you feel?

3. How do you think Adam and Eve felt?

4. God always keeps His promises. Sometimes it takes a long time, but He keeps them, just like His promise to Adam and Eve.

CAIN AND ABEL
Snow Shovel Trouble

Before long, Adam and Eve began to have children. When their first baby was born, they named him Cain. They named their second child Abel. Adam and Eve taught their two boys everything—how to walk, how to talk, how to skip stones on the clear lake, how to recognize the songs of different birds, and the leaves of different trees.

Most important, they taught Cain and Abel about God. Their stories from the Garden of Eden showed how much God loved them and how sad He was when they chose to listen to Satan.

Adam must have taken the boys to the gate of the Garden of Eden where they could see the angel guarding the way with a sword of fire. "Someday," Adam promised, "God will send a Savior who will die to pay for our sins. Then we can go back and live with God again."

Cain and Abel watched as Adam followed God's plan to remind them of the promise. Adam killed a lamb and placed it on an altar of stones. Then fire came down from God and burned up the sacrifice.

As Cain and Abel got older, they began to help their parents work. Adam and Eve had a garden where they grew grains and vegetables and fruits for the family to eat. They also had flocks of sheep, cattle, camels, and other animals to care for each day.

When they were young, the boys probably worked together to pick the corn or lead the sheep to water. But as time went by, Cain found that he loved gardening and growing things better. Abel found that he loved watching over the animals more.

One day after the two brothers were grown, the time came for Cain and Abel to bring their own sacrifice to God.

Abel selected the best and most perfect lamb he had raised to bring to the altar—just as his father had done. When the lamb's body was lying on the stones, God sent fire from heaven to burn it up. God was happy with Abel's sacrifice.

Cain knew that God asked for the sacrifice to remind them that a Savior was coming to die for their sins. But he didn't want to bring a lamb. He brought the best and most perfect vegetables and fruit from his garden. He laid these on the altar of stone.

But God was not happy with Cain's sacrifice. No fire came from heaven to burn it.

But instead of remembering how important it is to do what God asks, Cain got angry. "I worked just as hard to raise my vegetables as Abel did to raise his lamb," Cain said to himself. "My offering was just as good as his."

Abel came to talk to his brother, to help him understand why God could not accept his sacrifice. But Cain just got more and more angry. Finally, Cain was so mad that he killed his brother Abel.

God saw what Cain had done, and it made Him very, very sad. But He still loved Cain. He spoke to Cain to give him a chance to admit what he had done and be forgiven. God said, "Cain, where is your brother?"

Cain didn't admit anything. "How would I know? It's not my job to watch over him."

God could see that Cain wasn't sorry he had killed his brother. "Cain, I know what you did. From now on, the ground will not grow good crops for you. And you will have to wander around the world, never having a home to stay in."

Adam and Eve's hearts were broken to learn that Abel was dead and that Cain would never come home. But God blessed them, and soon they had another son named Seth. In fact, they had many more sons and daughters. And they taught each one about God's love and His plan to save them.

Snow Shovel Trouble

Ready for battle? Charge!"

Snowballs flew as DeeDee Adams and friends from her neighborhood launched another attack on the fort next door. "Take that!" DeeDee shouted as she tossed one of her snowballs over the fort wall. Suddenly, the boys in the fort stood and began firing back.

"Help! Retreat!" DeeDee shouted, ducking one snowball and outrunning another. She stopped behind a tree in her yard, panting and smiling.

"DeeDee," a voice called from right behind her.

Without even a thought, she whirled and threw her last snowball. *Smack!* It was a perfect hit . . . but on the wrong person.

"Oops. Sorry, Dad."

He brushed the snow off his coat. "That's OK. I should have known better than to walk into the middle of a battle. DeeDee, I need you to do something for me."

DeeDee looked around at her friends. "What is it?"

"I need you to shovel the snow off the sidewalk."

"Aw, Dad, do I have to?"

"DeeDee, you've had a good time out here playing. But your mother and I still have things to do to get ready for the meeting tonight. And since it's here at our house, we need the snow shoveled off the sidewalk."

DeeDee looked at the snow piled on the sidewalk. It wasn't too deep, but the sidewalk was long. She sighed and followed her dad to the garage.

"Use this big, flat shovel," he said, moving the rolled-up garden hose aside to grab it. "If you just push the snow instead of trying to pick it up, it won't be so hard. But be sure the sidewalk is clean. I don't want any of our guests to slip and fall."

DeeDee trudged out to the front, dragging the shovel along. It seemed a lot colder now than before. The snow battle had shifted farther down the street, so she could barely even see her friends.

"This is going to take forever," she said out loud. *Scru-u-unch.* She pushed the shovel against the snow. It cleared a short path. *Scru-u-unch.* She cleared another one.

Ten minutes of hard work didn't get DeeDee very far down the sidewalk. She dropped the shovel and sat down on the porch steps to rest. *I'm tired and I'm cold,* she thought.

Splat! The afternoon sun had melted an icicle on the roof's edge just enough to drip. DeeDee watched as another drop hit the bare circle on the step.

Hey, those water drops are clearing away the snow on the steps. I wish I could clear off the sidewalk that way. Then she remembered the garden hose in the garage. *I wonder . . .*

DeeDee hopped up and ran to get the hose. It was stiff with cold until she hooked it to the water faucet. After only a few minutes of spraying, all the snow on the sidewalk was gone.

As she coiled the hose back up to put it away, DeeDee was smiling. *I didn't shovel the sidewalk, but I sure cleared it off.* Then she ran down the street to join the battle.

That evening after dark, DeeDee helped her mother clear the dishes after supper. "Don't forget to turn on the porch light," Mrs. Adams reminded her husband.

Mr. Adams clicked the switch and looked out into the front yard. "The sidewalk is nice and clear. Thank you, DeeDee. It wasn't so hard, was it?"

DeeDee grinned. "It was much easier than I thought."

A few minutes later, the doorbell rang. It was Pastor Hill. "Welcome," Mr. Adams said as he opened the door. "Glad you could make it."

"It sure is slippery out there," Pastor Hill said as he wiped his boots.

"I know," Mr. Adams agreed. "The roads are dangerous."

Pastor Hill started to say more, but DeeDee's mother called to him from the other room.

DeeDee and her dad were watching from the window when the next car arrived. "It's Mr. and Mrs. Morton," DeeDee said. They watched as the couple began to walk up the sidewalk. Suddenly, Mrs. Morton's feet slipped, and she crashed down.

"Oh, no," Mr. Adams gasped. He raced out the door to help. As soon as he stepped onto the sidewalk, his feet flew up into the air.

DeeDee stared as he crashed down too. "Mom! Help!" she shouted as she ran to the door.

"Stop!" her dad said before she got off the porch. Her mom and Pastor Hill stopped right behind her. "The sidewalk is covered with ice. Pastor Hill, would you walk around through the snow and help the Mortons. I can make it back to the steps."

"Oh, no," DeeDee whispered. Suddenly, she felt like the sidewalk had jumped up and hit her in the stomach.

"DeeDee, what did you do to the sidewalk?" her dad asked as he finally stood up on the porch.

"I washed off the snow," DeeDee whispered.

"What did you say?"

There were tears in DeeDee's eyes as she watched Pastor Hill help Mrs. Morton back to her car. She took a deep breath. "I washed off the snow with the hose."

Her dad rubbed the bruise on his leg. "Why didn't you shovel it the way I told you? What were you thinking?"

DeeDee wiped at the tears on her face. "I didn't understand why I should shovel the snow if I knew a better way to get it off the sidewalk. I didn't know that it would turn to ice. I'm sorry!"

Later that night, Mrs. Adams hung up the phone. "Pastor Hill says that Mrs. Morton's leg isn't broken, only bruised. I guess it could have been a lot worse."

Mr. Adams agreed. He was resting on the couch. DeeDee was lying beside him. "DeeDee, what's your Sabbath School lesson about tomorrow?"

"Cain and Abel," DeeDee answered as she snuggled under his arm. "Abel offered his sacrifice the way God told them to. Cain wanted to do it his own way."

Mrs. Adams added, "Cain didn't know why he had to do it the way God told him to."

"So," DeeDee went on, "the lesson is, we show our love for God by doing what He asks, even when we don't understand why." Suddenly, she sat up. "Hey, Dad, you already taught me that lesson tonight."

Her dad grunted as he tried to sit up. "Now I know why I didn't want to be a teacher. It's too painful!"

DeeDee laughed and hugged him—carefully.

QUESTIONS

1. Do you ever get to play in snow? If you don't, which do you think would be the most fun—throwing snowballs, sledding, or making a snowman?

2. What should DeeDee have said to herself when she thought about using the water hose?

3. Why was Cain's way of sacrificing wrong?

4. Sometimes we don't understand why God asks us to do some things. If we love Him, what should we do?

THE FLOOD AND THE ARK
"Chicken"

Many, many years after Adam and Eve, the people of the world began to forget about God. Everywhere you looked, people were selfish, mean, and evil.

God looked at the world and saw that every person was wicked—every person except Noah. God's heart was filled with pain when He spoke to Noah. "Everywhere I look, people are filled with hate and violence. I'm going to have to destroy them—wipe them all off of the earth and start over. So I want you to build a big boat—an ark—for you and your family."

Noah's eyes got really big. "A boat? God, are you sure? There's not enough water around here to make a big boat float."

God was sure. "Noah, I am going to destroy the world with a flood. If you do what I ask, you and your family will be saved."

Noah must have pinched himself to be sure he wasn't

dreaming. "But God, are you sure? I don't know how to build a big boat like that."

God was sure. "Noah, I will tell you exactly how to build it. Use cypress wood to make it four hundred and fifty feet long, with one big door in the side and a window going around the top."

Noah must have asked, "God, are you sure? My family is not that big."

God was sure. "The ark has to be big because it is going to carry two of every kind of bird and animal— seven of every kind of animal that you can eat. They will fill the earth again after the flood."

So Noah began the job God had given him. He gathered the wood and began to build the ark. Before long, a crowd of people gathered to see what he was doing. "What is it?" they asked. "The biggest house in the world?"

Noah stopped hammering and shook his head. "No, it's a boat. There's going to be a flood."

Everyone who heard him laughed. "Ha! You must be crazy, Noah. A flood big enough to float a boat that big would cover everything!"

"That's right," Noah said, "God is sending a flood to clean the whole world. Only people who are on this boat—this ark—will be saved. Please, come and join me and my family and be safe from the flood."

The people only laughed harder. "You really are crazy if you think your God could flood the whole world. That's not even possible!"

But Noah kept building, and whenever a crowd would

gather, he would preach to them about the coming flood. "Give up your wicked ways and follow God," he would say. "The flood is coming! You must come into the ark to be safe!"

But the people only laughed at him.

As the years went by, Noah's sons grew up, and they helped him build the ark also. Finally, one day, there was no building left to do. The ark was finished.

Then God spoke to Noah again. "Gather the animals into the ark," He said. "It's almost time for the flood."

Noah asked, "Are you sure, God? It will take a long time to gather all those animals."

God was sure. "Look, Noah," was all He said.

And Noah looked out and saw long lines of animals walking toward the ark. Two by two and seven by seven, the animals and birds moved right up the ramp and through the door into the ark. Parrots, ferrets, baboons, raccoons, kangaroos and bandicoots—they came flying, hopping, slinking, and trotting to the space Noah and his sons had built for each one.

Then God spoke again. "Now, Noah, move your family into the ark. It's almost time."

This time, Noah didn't ask any questions. He moved his family into the ark, then stopped and spoke to the crowd that had gathered to watch. Once more, he said, "The flood is coming. Please, come into the ark and be saved."

But no one would listen. They just kept laughing. "Noah, you said you were building a boat. It looks more like you were building a zoo! And your family must be going into the last cage!"

Sadly, Noah turned and followed his family into the ark. Then God closed the big door behind him. For seven days they waited, but nothing happened. Outside, the people laughed and shouted even louder.

But on the eighth day, something did happen. Black clouds filled the sky, and fat raindrops hit the top of the ark. The rain began to fall faster and harder until it seemed like the sky had turned into a waterfall.

Now the people outside the ark weren't laughing. They were shouting for someone to open the door and let them into the ark. But it was too late.

Noah wasn't laughing either. He was crying for the people who wouldn't choose to be saved—and so was God.

The rain kept falling, and the water got deeper. Soon it was higher than the buildings and towers. When all the valleys were filled, the ark began to float. And the floodwaters kept rising higher and higher. Finally, all the waters of the earth crashed together, and the flood covered even the mountains.

And every living thing that breathed air died.

"Chicken"

The flood is coming! You must come into the ark to be safe!" A man in a long gray beard sat in front of the ark and preached to the rowdy crowd in front of him.

"You must be crazy," someone in the crowd said. "No

one believes in floods. Come on and join our party."

Another person in the crowd spoke. "Mrs. Shue, do you think they really called Noah names like that?"

The Shoebox Kids were studying the story of Noah. Willie sat in front of a big sign that said "ARK." With a long gray beard hanging from his chin, he looked like Noah.

"Yes, I think they did, DeeDee," Mrs. Shue answered. "They did everything they could to make him give up on following God."

"It would have been hard to keep preaching if every-one was making fun of you," Chris said.

Willie pulled the beard down. "If he asked God to help him, I'm sure it was easy. After all, he was a real follower of God. He was building the ark."

"I'm not sure it was easy," Mrs. Shue said. "But Noah did preach, and his family was saved in the ark."

I think it would be pretty easy, Willie said to himself. *After all, Noah knew he was doing the right thing.*

The next week, Willie finished his lunch early and rolled into the school store. It was crowded, so Willie waited his turn with three other kids from his class.

"Hi, Charles," Willie said. "What are you here for?"

Charles held up a candy bar. "We're getting dessert. You too?"

"No, I have to get some paper. Mom decided it was easier just to give me the money to buy it here." While Willie talked, he noticed that Avery and Jon were whisper-ing to each other and poking Charles. *It would be nice to hang around with these guys and have things to whisper about,* he thought.

"May I help you?"

Willie looked up and smiled at the store clerk. "Yes, Mrs. Myers. I need a package of paper."

"Which size?" she asked.

While Mrs. Myers turned around show him the different packages of papers, Willie heard more whispering from behind him. Soon, he had his paper and headed down the hall towards his classroom.

"Hey, Willie, wait up." Willie stopped and waited for Charles and his friends. "Here, we got a candy bar for you while we were at it."

"Thanks," Willie said. He was really surprised. *Maybe Charles wants to be friends too.*

"Are you going by the school store tomorrow?" Charles asked as they went on toward the classroom.

Willie shrugged. "I don't know. I don't think I need anything else."

"Why don't you get some pencils or something," Charles suggested. "We'll meet you there again."

As he went to his desk, Willie was smiling. *I could hang around with them every day after lunch. That would be fun.*

The next day, Willie joined his friends at the store. "I need pencils today, Mrs. Myers," he said cheerfully. This time, he waited at the door while Charles paid for his candy bar.

"Great," Charles said as the group headed down the hall, "another good dessert day." Willie watched in surprise as all three boys pulled out candy bars and ripped open the wrappers.

"Chicken"

"Hey, where did you get . . . oh, you must have brought them from home," Willie said.

Charles pulled out another candy bar and tossed it to Willie. "No," he said, "we got them from the store."

Willie stopped. "But I saw you pay for one candy bar. And you have four."

Avery and Jon snickered. Charles rolled his eyes. "We only paid for one. The others we stuck in our pockets while Mrs. Myers was helping you. That's why we got one for you—because you helped."

Willie's mouth fell open. "But that's stealing!"

All three of them laughed out loud. "Not really," Charles said. "This is our school, so those candy bars belong to us. Don't you agree?"

Willie gulped. "Well, I . . ."

"You're not a chicken, are you?" Jon asked. "Are you afraid of getting caught?"

"No, I . . ."

"You're not a goody-goody, are you?" Avery snorted. "Someone who thinks they never do anything wrong? And thinks they're better than everyone else?"

Willie stammered, "N-no."

"Good," Charles said. "See you at lunch tomorrow."

Willie just sat there in the hall for a minute. He stared at the candy bar in his hands. *But I don't want to steal. I know that's not right. Why didn't I tell them that?* Suddenly, he remembered the story of Noah. *I guess I was wrong. I thought it would be easy to do what's right.*

The next day, Willie's prayer before he ate took longer than usual. *God,* he said silently, *help me be honest and truthful, no matter what Charles and those guys say. Help me be as faithful as Noah. Oh, and thank you for the food. Amen.*

Charles and his friends were waiting outside the lunchroom door. "Well, are you ready to go shopping?" Charles asked.

Willie shook his head. "No. I'm not doing that again."

"You really are a chicken," Jon said.

"No," Willie answered. "But I am a Christian. And I know it's wrong to steal."

"A Christian?" Avery threw up his hands. "So you think you're some kind of holy guy? You think you're better than us?"

"No," Willie tried to explain. "I just . . ."

"Are you coming with us or not?" Charles asked.

Willie took a deep breath and shook his head again. "No. In fact, I'm going in there to pay Mrs. Myers for the two candy bars you gave me."

Charles leaned close to Willie's face. "You'd better not tell how you got them."

"Don't worry," Willie said, "that's your problem. I'm just doing what I know is right."

"Come on, guys. Let's get out of here." Charles led his friends away.

Willie rolled toward the store. He didn't have any friends to hang around with that day, but he felt a lot happier. He even started to whistle.

QUESTIONS

1. What do you think was harder for Noah to do—

build the ark, or listen to people make fun of him?

2. Have you ever been tempted to steal from a store? It makes Jesus sad, and it's against the law!

3. How do you feel when someone calls you a chicken, or a goody-goody? Do you let what someone says change your mind about how you act?

4. God helped Noah be a faithful follower, even when people laughed at him. God will help you too, if you ask!

7
CHAPTER

THE PROMISE OF A NEW WORLD
Facts Don't Lie

Now the ark was bobbing up and down in the wild water. The storm was so great that the angels had to keep the ark safe and steady. For forty days and nights the rain kept falling.

Then God sent a strong wind to dry the earth. It blew for many days, and the floodwater began to go down. After two more months of floating, the ark bumped onto dry ground and rested on the mountains of Ararat.

One of Noah's sons must have said, "Father, we've all tired of being on this boat. Is it safe to go out now?"

Noah shook his head. "Soon, but not yet," he answered, "And remember, God closed the big door when we came inside. We'll have to wait for Him to open it before we can go out. But let's try to find out if any dry land is out there. Go and bring me one of the ravens."

Then Noah opened the window at the top of the ark and let the raven fly out. It flew in big circles around the ark, but then it came back to the window. "There must be no place for it to land," Noah reported. "We'll have to wait longer."

A week later, they tried it again. This time, Noah sent out a dove. But there was still no place for it to land, so it came back to the ark. Noah shook his head. "Soon, but not yet," he told his sons again.

Another week went by. Everyone watched as Noah let the dove fly free from the window again. This time it came back with an olive leaf in its beak!

Noah held up the leaf to show everyone. "You know what this means, don't you?" he shouted. "There's dry land, and things are beginning to grow again!"

Everyone wanted to know, "When can we go out? When can we leave the ark?"

Noah had to shake his head. "Soon, but not yet," he said.

They waited another week. Then Noah let the dove fly out the window again. They waited and waited, but the dove didn't return. Noah was happy. "There must be enough trees growing that the dove feels it can make a home," he said. "And there must be a lot of ground showing to grow that many trees."

"So, when can we go and see those trees?" everyone asked. "When can we go out?"

"Soon," Noah said, "but not yet. There have to be enough dry and growing things to feed all the animals when we leave the ark. God will know when the time is right."

And so they waited, and waited, and waited some more. They waited fifty-seven more days until the all the land was dry again. Then God spoke to Noah, "It's time for you and your family to leave the ark. Take all the animals and birds out also, so they can go and fill the earth with their children."

Then the door opened, and everyone raced out. Those people and those animals had been inside the ark for more than a year!

But the world they found was very different from the one they remembered. Now there were rugged, rocky mountains. Now there were places of deep ice and snow. Now there were deep oceans that seemed to stretch out forever. It seemed as though the whole world had been turned upside down and shaken. Nothing was the same as it had been before.

As the animals scattered to find their new homes, Noah built an altar and offered a sacrifice to God. "Thank you, God," Noah prayed, "for saving us from the flood and giving us a fresh new world."

God was happy with Noah and his family. "I will never destroy the earth with a flood again," He promised. "And to remind you of My promise, I'm putting My rainbow in the clouds. Whenever you see My rainbow, you will remember My promise."

Facts Don't Lie

You really believe that?"

Willie Teller felt his face turning red. It seemed as though everyone in the class was laughing at him—even Mr. Hunt.

"Now, class," Mr. Hunt said, "if Willie chooses to, he

can believe in the story of Noah's flood. But the truth is, scientific facts show that the world has existed for millions and millions of years and that there was no such thing as a worldwide flood."

"Come on, Willie," Charles said, "why would you believe that Bible story when the facts say it's wrong? Facts don't lie."

"B-because the Bible says so," Willie stammered. "It says that God created the world and that there was a flood. It's in my Bible lesson this week."

"Do you believe in the Easter bunny too?" someone said with a snicker.

Mr. Hunt held up his hand. "It's OK for Willie to believe what he chooses to. But, class, you can see that if you don't stick with the scientific facts, any crazy idea might seem OK."

Willie sank down as low as he could in his chair.

At home that afternoon, Willie was trying to think of something to do instead of homework. Then he heard his dad's voice.

"Willie, come out here for a minute."

"Coming," he called back. But when he stuck his head out the back door, no one was there. "Dad?" No one answered. *Maybe he's out in the front yard,* Willie thought.

He rolled to the front door. "Dad?" No one answered, but he heard noises by the driveway. As he rolled off the porch, the noises got louder.

Arf! Arf!

Then Willie heard his dad's voice. He was shouting. "Coco, stop! Coco, come back!"

Willie's dog appeared around the side of the house. Coco hadn't noticed the funny gray mud he ran right through to get to Willie.

"Coco, get down," Willie said as the dog tried to jump up on his lap. "What do you have all over your feet?"

Mr. Teller appeared around the corner. "Wet cement," he said to answer Willie's question. "And look at my new sidewalk."

Willie rolled closer to see a new sidewalk stretching from the edge of the driveway around the back of the house. There were dog prints all the way across one section.

"This is what I wanted you to see," Mr. Teller said. "When I heard you call from the back, I opened the gate on this side. Coco jumped out and did just what I was afraid he would do. Come here, you crazy mutt, so I can rinse off your feet."

"Dad, can you fix it?"

Mr. Teller led Coco back to the backyard. "It's still soft enough to smooth over again," he said over his shoulder.

A few minutes later, Willie watched as his dad smoothed out Coco's tracks with a trowel. Suddenly, Willie blurted out a question. "Dad, is the story of Noah's flood just a fairy tale?" He rushed on before his dad had a chance to answer. "My teacher told us that scientific facts prove that the earth wasn't created like the Bible says and that there was no worldwide flood."

Mr. Teller finished smoothing and set the trowel down. "Willie, I had these same questions when I was young. I did some studying and found some answers you might be interested in. You wait here and guard our cement. I want to find some things in the garage."

Willie waited until his dad came out carrying a post-card and a rock. "Look at this," Mr. Teller said, pointing to the postcard. "It's a picture of the Grand Canyon in Arizona. It's a mile deep, so you can see the layers of rocks under the ground."

"Wow," Willie whispered. "Are those striped rocks?"

"Yes," Mr. Teller said. "The rock layers were laid down like mud on the bottom of a lake. One layer on top of the other was left behind, like frosting on a chocolate cake."

"How?"

"Many scientists think it took millions of years."

Willie frowned. "So the story of the Flood isn't true."

"I didn't say that," his dad answered. "Look at this." He pointed to a thick brown stripe of rock on the canyon wall. "See the white stripe on top? See how the white stripe fits on top of the brown one smooth and flat, like a white cover on a brown book?"

"Yes. So?"

Mr. Teller tried to explain. "Scientists think that the brown layer formed, then fifteen million years went by before the white rock was laid on top of it."

"Are they right?"

Mr. Teller smiled. "How long do you think we could keep this concrete nice and smooth if it stayed wet?"

Willie laughed. "We couldn't even keep Coco out of it for ten minutes."

"What if it were soft for a year? Could we keep it smooth?"

"No way!"

Mr. Teller agreed. "You're right. But think about those rock layers again. When the brown layer was laid down, it was soft for a while. And even after it was hard, rain and wind would be wearing it down to make it rough and unleveled. But scientists think it sat there for fifteen million years—and it was still nice and smooth and level when the white layer was formed on top."

"That doesn't make sense," Willie said. "It should have been worn down in lots of places by then."

"It makes a lot more sense to think that those two layers were laid down one right after the other when a big flood stirred up a lot of mud."

"That's right!" Willie agreed. "And that's just what Noah's flood would have done. So some of the scientific facts support the story from the Bible."

"Here's another scientific fact," Mr. Teller said, holding out the rock. "I picked this up on top of a mountain."

Willie looked at the rock carefully. "Hey, this rock has seashells in it. It has to be from the ocean."

Mr. Teller explained. "When this rock's layer was formed, it was under water. So either the mountain was covered with water or—"

"Like during Noah's flood," Willie interrupted.

"—Or," Mr. Teller went on, "that layer used to be at the bottom of the ocean, but it was pushed up to become a mountain. In fact, scientists have found water-formed rocks and shells on mountains in countries all over the world. You can even find them on Mount Everest, the highest mountain in the world."

"So," Willie said, "either water covered all the mountains or something must have turned this world inside out. Either way, this scientific fact helps prove the story of Noah's flood."

Mr. Teller just nodded and smiled.

Willie was thinking ahead. "Dad, can I take the postcard and the rock to school tomorrow? Maybe I can teach my class something about scientific facts. After all, facts don't lie."

QUESTIONS

1. Have you ever been teased at school for being a Christian or for believing the Bible?

2. Have you ever watched someone pour fresh cement? Have you ever been allowed to write your name or initials in it?

3. Some people think that all scientific facts say that the Bible isn't true. Now you know that some scientific facts say that the story of Noah's flood is true!

4. What promise do you remember when you see a rainbow?

CHAPTER

THE TOWER OF BABEL
Maria's Blaster Disaster

As the years went by, Noah's sons—Ham, Shem, and Japheth—had children of their own. And their children had children until there were many people on the world again. But instead of spreading all around the world like God wanted them to, many of the people stayed together and built big cities.

One group moved to the flat plain of Babylonia and learned to make bricks out of the clay there. So they began to build a big city. And these people stopped listening to God. Since they didn't want to hear the truth about God and His love, Satan tricked them into being afraid of God. They didn't believe God's rainbow promise and worried that God would send another flood to destroy them.

"Let's build a tower," the people decided. "We'll build it so tall that even if God sends a flood, we'll be safe. We'll build it until it reaches the clouds! We'll build it until it reaches heaven!"

"That's right," others agreed. "If we build a tower like that, we'll be famous all over the world. We'll build a famous city and stay here forever."

God came down to see this city and its big tower. God loved these people just the way He loved those who didn't choose to get on the ark. He wanted to save them if He could. "If they stay here building this city and this tower," God said, "they will only grow more selfish until they are as evil as the people before the flood."

God decided on a simple plan. "I will confuse their language," He said. And He did. One day, the people woke up and found that they couldn't understand one another. The brick makers couldn't understand the brick carriers. The builders working on the walls couldn't understand the builders working on the windows.

Before long, all the work was stopped. Everyone looked for others they could talk to and understand. Then groups of people who spoke the same language began to move away from the city to start their own little farms and villages.

From then on, the tall tower was called the Tower of Babel, because *babel* means confusion. And that's what God did—He confused their languages. Then they scattered around the world just as He had planned.

Maria's Blaster Disaster

I can't believe it!"

Maria Vargas looked up from her bowl of cereal as her dad came in from the garage. He wasn't happy at all.

"It's fairly warm today, so I opened up my little hot-house for ten minutes," he explained. "The next thing I knew, that cat from next door was in my tomato plants!"

Maria had watched her dad build his little hothouse out beside the garage. It was square frame of wood with plastic tacked over it. "It keeps the plants warm so they can begin to grow before spring comes," Mr. Vargas had explained. "When it's warm outside, I'll plant them in the garden."

Mrs. Vargas patted her husband's arm. "Did your plants get knocked over?"

Mr. Vargas sat down. "No, the cat only dug up one plant. But that's one too many. If I'm going to have toma-toes to show at the fair this summer, I've got to get them growing early. And if that cat kills them, I'll kill—"

"No, dear," Mrs. Vargas said, "let's not threaten small animals. I'm sure your tomato plants will be fine."

"Daddy," Yoyo asked with her mouth half full of oatmeal, "why are you growing tomatoes in a house?"

Mr. Vargas smiled. "I'll grow them in their little house when they're tiny, Yoyo. When they get bigger, I'll plant them outside."

Yoyo turned to Maria. "When they're big enough, they get to go outside and play," she explained.

Maria tried not to laugh with her mouth full. *Dad sure did get mad at that cat,* she thought. *I sure wouldn't want him to get mad at me.*

Mr. Vargas wasn't through. "Yoyo, I want you to stay away from my hothouse." He looked at Maria and Chris. "I want all of you to play on the other side of the yard. If those plants are damaged now, I won't be able to grow any big tomatoes in time for the fair."

Later that afternoon, Maria walked by the living room on her way outside. Her mother was visiting with Mrs. Myers from down the street. Maria stopped to hear what they were saying.

"Emily doesn't really have a family," Mrs. Myers said. "She's been out on her own for a long time. Her father threw her out of the house."

"He made her leave?" Mrs. Vargas asked.

"Yes," Mrs. Myers answered sadly. "Even though she was his daughter, he was too mad to ever forgive her. They haven't spoken in years."

Maria backed away. *Emily's father got mad and wouldn't forgive her,* she thought. *I'll never make my father mad like that.* When she thought about what Mrs. Myers had said, it reminded her of her Sabbath School lesson the week before.

When Noah was alive, people made God mad, and He sent the flood to get rid of them, Maria remembered. *I hope He doesn't get mad at me.*

Later that week, Maria was out in the yard playing with her soccer ball. With spring coming, she wanted to practice. "Hey, Yoyo, watch this," she called. With a mighty kick, she smacked the ball across the yard.

Yoyo chased after it. "Watch this," she called. Her kick sent the ball rolling toward the back porch.

"I'll get it," Maria called. She smacked it back toward Yoyo. Yoyo's next kick sent the ball around the corner by the garage. Maria was right behind it. "I'll show you my best kick—my Blaster."

Maria's Blaster Disaster

Stepping around her dad's hothouse, Maria lined the ball up and got ready for another big kick. "Here comes my Blaster," she shouted. She thought about what her father had said and almost didn't kick it. *I want to show Yoyo my Blaster kick. I won't hit the hothouse.*

She kicked it harder than ever before. *Smack! Crack!* Plastic and dirt flew everywhere.

Maria almost stopped breathing. She ran to the hothouse. "Oh, no. Oh, no. Oh, no." She moved the plastic wrap and saw the tomato plants. The little pots were all knocked over. The dirt was scattered. And the little plants were broken.

"I don't see the ball," Yoyo called from across the yard. "Maria, did you kick yet?"

Dad's going to kill me! Maria scooped the dirt back into the pots. She tried to stand up the broken plants. Then she set the broken frame and plastic back around it.

"Maria?" Yoyo showed up around the corner. "What happened to Dad's hothouse?"

"Nothing," Maria said as she quickly stood up. "It's fine. Come on, let's play." She kicked the ball and ran after it, pretending that nothing was wrong. But as hard as she ran, she couldn't forget what was waiting around that corner when her dad came home.

"I'm going in," she called to Yoyo a few minutes later. "I don't feel so good. I think I'll lie down for a while." But even lying down on her bed with her pillow on her head didn't help.

"Maria, are you feeling OK?" It was Mrs. Vargas. Before Maria could answer, they both heard Mr. Vargas's voice at the back door.

"What happened to my tomatoes?"

Maria rolled over against the wall.

Mrs. Vargas almost whispered. "Maria, you didn't break Daddy's hothouse, did you?"

The pillow nodded. "And I know Dad hates me now," Maria sniffled. Her mom started to say something, but she left quietly. Maria clenched her fists and waited. Finally, she heard it.

"Maria."

It was her father. She pushed the pillow away and sat up. "I'm sorry about the tomato plants," she cried. Tears ran down her face. "Do I have to leave now?"

Her father walked across the room and sat down beside her. Maria took a deep breath and closed her eyes. Then it happened.

Her dad's arms wrapped around her in a big hug. "Maria, you're not leaving. I'm keeping you with me forever."

Maria's eyes popped open. "You don't hate me?"

"Maria, I love you." Her dad stroked her hair. "Nothing you can do will ever change that. I'm very unhappy that my tomato plants are dead. I'm unhappy that you disobeyed. But that doesn't change how much I love you."

Suddenly, Maria didn't feel sick at all. She did get to help rebuild the hothouse and do dishes every night for a week. But at the end of the week, she was still smiling.

At the Shoebox, Mrs. Shue told the story of the Tower of Babel. "The people were disobeying God, as the people before the Flood had. And just as God loved the people who didn't choose to get on the ark, He loved the people at Babel. These stories tell us that no matter what we do, our heavenly Father still loves us."

Maria understood better than anyone else did.

QUESTIONS

1. Have you ever planted tomatoes? Have you ever raised plants in a hothouse?

2. How do you feel when someone is mad at you?

3. Sometimes, if you do something wrong, does it feel as though no one loves you?

4. Did you know that God always loves you, no matter what you do?

CHAPTER 9

ABRAM FOLLOWS GOD
Chris's Crazy Ball

After God confused the language of people at the Tower of Babel, the people scattered to smaller towns and cities. One of those cities was called Ur. The people of Ur, already confused by Satan, worshiped many different gods. But one man—Abram—and his family worshiped the One True God. And God had a special plan for them.

God spoke to Abram. "I want you to leave this city and go to a land that I will lead you to."

Abram knew God's voice, but he didn't know where they were going. But his whole family believed in God so they packed up and moved with him—his wife, Sarai, his father, Terah, his brother Tahor, his nephew Lot, and all the family's servants.

They packed all of their things on a long line of camels and headed across the desert. Their sheep and goats were herded along behind. They traveled for many days until they reached the city of Haran.

Abram's family settled in Haran for a long time. After Abram's father, Terah, died, God spoke to Abram again.

"Leave this city," God said, "and your father's family and go to a place I will show you. There I will make your children into a mighty nation, and you will be famous across the world. And everyone in the world will be blessed because of you."

So Abram left Haran and all of his relatives. Only his wife Sarai and his nephew Lot left with him. They packed up all that they owned and traveled to the place God showed Abram—the Land of Canaan.

When they arrived at a place called Shechem, God said, "I will give all of this land to your children and their children."

Abram was a little surprised to hear this, because he was seventy-five years old, and he and Sarai didn't have any children. But he had faith in God, and he thought, *Maybe now God plans to give us children.*

The Canaanites who lived in the land worshiped many gods, so Abram built an altar at Shechem to teach them about the true God. After that, the family traveled to a place where the flocks could graze near Bethel. Abram built another altar there. Everywhere they traveled in Canaan, Abram built an altar and praised God.

Later, a famine came to Canaan—a time when no rain fell so no food could grow. Abram and his family traveled to Egypt and stayed there for a time. When they traveled back to Canaan, both Abram and Lot had more gold, more silver, and more flocks of cattle and sheep.

Before long, the shepherds who watched Lot's flocks

began to argue with the shepherds who watched Abram's flocks. "This pasture of grass is for our cattle," one would say. "Keep yours away." Or "This well only has enough water for our sheep," another would say. "Stay back."

Finally, Abram met with Lot at the top of a small mountain to discuss it. "There's no need for our people to fight," Abram said. "There is plenty of room for us to spread out. Why don't you take your flocks and your people in one direction, and I will take mine in another."

From where they stood on the mountain, they could see a long way. On one side was the beautiful green valley of the Jordan River and the city of Sodom. On the other side were brown and green hills and deserts. Even though Abram was older and had taken care of Lot for most of his life, he let Lot choose first.

Lot looked at the soft green land near the river and the big city. Then he looked at the hills and deserts. It was easy to see which was a nicer place to live. "I'll take the river valley," he said.

So Abram moved his tents and his family and his flocks away from the green valley to the hills. And there, God spoke to him again.

"Look north," God said. "Look south. Look east and west. I am going to give all the land that you can see to your children. And your family will be so big, it will be just as easy to count all the pieces of dust in the world as it will be to count your family."

And even though Abram still didn't have any children, he believed God. He had faith in the God who had become his Friend.

Chris's Crazy Ball

Come see what I bought!"

Chris Vargas's shout brought his sisters running to the kitchen. "What is it?" Yoyo asked.

"Oh, it's just another ball," Maria complained.

Chris laughed. "No, it's not just another ball. It's different. Watch this." He set the big blue ball down on the kitchen floor and kicked it toward Maria.

Boing! The ball bounced to Yoyo.

"Hey! How did you do that?" Yoyo almost shouted.

"It's a Crazy Ball," Chris explained. "It turns and twists while it's bouncing and rolling. You never know where it's going to go."

"Let me try it," Maria demanded. She tried to bounce the ball back to Chris.

Boing! It hit the floor and bounced right to her mother.

"Hey, take this game outside," Mrs. Vargas said.

"Come on, let's play soccer with it," Chris shouted as he headed out. Maria and Yoyo were right behind him.

They kicked and shouted in the front yard as the ball went everywhere but where they kicked it. "Did you see that?" Chris pointed to the edge of the sidewalk that was their goal. "The ball went right up to the goal, then, '*boing*,' it bounced away."

After a while, Maria got bored. "Let's play something else. How about kickball? That would be fun with this Crazy Ball."

Chris thought about it. "No, it's too windy. Let's keep playing soccer." He dribbled the ball across the yard.

"I want to play kickball too," Yoyo said.

"Come on, Chris," Maria added. "We've played soccer long enough."

Chris shook his head. "It's my ball, and I want to play soccer." He kicked the ball, and it bounced past his sisters. "That's another goal for me. You guys better start playing or you're going to lose."

Yoyo shoved her hands in her pockets. "I'm cold," she said. "I'm going in." She ran to the door.

Maria looked at Chris. He was chasing the ball again. "I'm going in too," she muttered. And she followed Yoyo inside.

Fine, Chris said to himself when they left, *I'll play by myself.* He kicked the ball against the garage door.

Boing! It bounced away toward the rose bushes.

This is more fun than playing kickball with them anyway, Chris told himself. But he didn't play very long.

After school the next day, Chris grabbed his Crazy Ball and called to his mom, "I'm going over to play at Ryan's house."

"Be back by supper time," she answered.

Ryan thought the Crazy Ball was great. "Let me try it," he said.

Boing! The ball bounced and headed right back at Ryan.

"Whoa!" Ryan shouted. "This ball is crazy."

"Come on," Chris called, "let's play soccer with it." They each picked a goal to defend and started kicking. The ball went everywhere except where they wanted it to go.

"Hey, come back here!"

"Stop that ball!"

After a few minutes, Ryan fell on the ball, and Chris plopped down beside him. "This Crazy Ball is really fun, Chris," Ryan said, breathing hard. "I know—let's try playing basketball with it."

Chris shook his head. "No, I want to keep playing soccer." He jumped up. "Let's go."

Ryan didn't jump up so fast. "I'm tired of running back and forth. Let's just take turns shooting at the basket."

Chris tapped the ball out from under Ryan's arm and jumped up. "I'm headed for your goal," he shouted over his shoulder.

Ryan didn't move. "Come on, let's play basketball," he called.

Chris shook his head. "It's my ball, and I want to play soccer."

"Fine," Ryan answered, "but I don't." Then he got up and went into his house.

Chris picked up his ball and headed home. *I don't need Ryan to have fun,* he thought. *I just want to play soccer.* In his own yard, he spotted Maria and Yoyo playing with their dolls.

"Come on, girls," he called as he kicked the ball toward them. "Let's play."

Boing! The ball bounced in front of them, then headed toward the porch.

"I'll play kickball if you want," Maria called back.

"Me too," Yoyo agreed.

Chris shook his head. "I want to play soccer."

"Well, we don't," Maria said. "We'll just keep playing dolls. Right, Yoyo?"

"Right."

"Fine," Chris muttered to himself. "I don't need them to have fun." He bounced the ball against the garage door again. But this time it wasn't much fun to chase the ball all by himself.

Finally, he grabbed the ball and stomped into the kitchen. "Mom, I'm bored."

His mother looked up from a bowl of sliced carrots. "Even with a new ball, you're bored? Why?"

"No one will play with me," Chris complained.

Mrs. Vargas raised one eyebrow. "Didn't Ryan want to play?"

"Yeah, he doesn't want to play soccer anymore. He just wanted to play basketball. So he went in."

Mrs. Vargas looked at Chris but didn't say anything.

"And Maria and Yoyo will only play kickball. So there's no one for me to play with," Chris finished.

"You mean, no one wants to play what you want to play," Mrs. Vargas said.

"Well, it's my ball. And I only want to play soccer." Chris folded his arms. "I can do what I want to, right?"

Mrs. Vargas nodded. "That's right. It's your ball. If you choose only to play soccer with it, no one will make you do something else. But remember, everyone else can choose too. And I guess they choose not to play soccer. So where does that leave you?"

Chris's arms dropped. "With no one to play with."

"It's OK for you to choose what you want to do or

play. But if you aren't going to be selfish, you have to put others first sometimes. Being like Jesus doesn't mean always having to do what anyone else wants to do. But it does mean sharing and caring about what others want."

Chris looked sad. "Maria and Yoyo and Ryan all played soccer with me for a while. I guess I could have played something else with them. But I didn't feel like doing what they wanted, Mom."

She patted Chris on the arm. "God will help you put others first, if you ask Him."

That Sabbath, the Shoebox lesson was about Abram and Lot. "Lot put what he wanted first, instead of thinking about Abram. Does anyone know what happens when you put yourself first?" Mrs. Shue asked.

Chris knew—but he let the others raise their hands first.

QUESTIONS

1. What happens when you put yourself first?

2. What happened to Chris when he put what he wanted first?

3. It's important to remember that you are a special person and you should be able to choose things to do. But it's just as important to share and care about others. So remember to do both!

4. If it's hard for you to let others go first, remember to ask God for help. He's always ready to help you.

10
CHAPTER

ABRAM RESCUES LOT
Two Dimes and a Nickel

As he always did, Abram built an altar when he moved to the hills. He settled near a place called Mamre, and soon his neighbors knew about the God that Abram worshiped. Three of his neighbors were princes—rulers of the lands they lived on.

In those days, there were a lot of wars and battles between the kings and princes in Canaan. Each one was trying to take over the other king's lands and riches.

Abram's neighbors soon saw that even though Abram had enough people to make a powerful army, he was a good man, and he could be trusted not to attack them. They said to Abram, "Let's agree to help each other. If we have trouble, you promise to help us. If you have trouble, we promise to help you."

Abram agreed, and before long he was glad that he did.

The king of Elam attacked the king of Sodom and captured the city and area around it. He took the people of Sodom away to be slaves and took all of their gold, silver, flocks, and treasures.

Lot and his family were captured also. Everything they owned was taken, and they were led away to be slaves.

One of Lot's servants escaped and traveled all the way to Abram's tents. He rushed in to report to Abram. "Your nephew Lot has been captured by the King of Elam!"

Abram could have said, "It's not my problem. Lot chose Sodom and the best land for himself, and now he's getting what he deserves." But he didn't. Abram had learned a lot about love and forgiveness from God, and he knew that he should help Lot.

He gathered all his men who had been trained to fight. Then he sent messages to his neighbors and asked for their help. Soon Abram was leading a small army after the king of Elam.

After dark, Abram divided his army into small groups. Then they surprised the enemy by attacking from all sides at once. The enemy soldiers ran away, and Abram won the battle!

Then Abram brought all the captured people and all the gold and treasures and flocks that had been stolen back to Sodom. The king of Sodom and Melchizedek (mel-KIZ-uh-dek), the king of Salem came out to meet him.

Melchizedek was also a follower of the true God—he was a priest and a king. He said to Abram, "You will be blessed by the true God who created the world. Let's thank and praise Him for helping you defeat your enemies."

In those days, if you defeated an enemy in a battle

like Abram had done, you got to keep all the treasures you captured. And the people too, if you wanted.

So Abram could have kept it all. But instead, he gave Melchizedek one-tenth of everything he brought back from the battle. Abram gave one-tenth to the priest as an offering to God. Abram knew that giving one-tenth of his money is called giving tithe. By giving tithe, Abram was showing everyone that he knew God had helped him defeat the enemy.

Then the king of Sodom said, "Keep all the gold, silver, and flocks you brought back from the battle. But, please, give the people of Sodom back to me."

But Abraham didn't want anything to do with the evil king of Sodom. "I promise God," Abram said, "in front of all these people, that I will not keep one thing of Sodom's—not one string, or thread, or sandal strap. I don't want you to say that you made me rich."

Abram added, "I won't take anything but the food my men have already eaten. But give my three neighbors their share for helping me."

So Abram gave everything left back to the king of Sodom. All the people of Sodom saw what kind of person Abram was. And they learned about the God he worshiped. By being honest and giving tithe, Abram taught all the kings and peoples in Canaan about God.

Two Dimes and a Nickel

Here you go. One dollar, two dollars, one quarter, two dimes, and one nickel."

ABRAM RESCUES LOT

Jenny Wallace watched while her neighbor Mrs. Garrison counted the money out into her hand. Her mind was already racing through ideas of what she could buy.

"Thanks again for helping me clean out my garage," Mrs. Garrison added. "You'll come back and help me when I have my garage sale, won't you?"

"I will," Jenny promised. "See you later." She skipped home and burst into the kitchen. "Mom! When can we go to the store?"

"Whoa," Mrs. Wallace said. "What's the big rush? What's happening at the store?"

Jenny rolled her eyes. "Mom, nothing's happening at the store. Mrs. Garrison paid me for helping her. Now I have money to spend. See?"

Her mom looked over the bills and coins and nodded. "Very good. You must have been a real help to her. So what do you want to buy?"

"I'm not sure. Maybe one of those tiny little dolls I saw—or a detective note pad and spyglass. Or something else!"

"OK, OK," Mrs. Wallace said with a laugh. "We need to go to the grocery store later, so we'll stop by ShopTown on our way."

Jenny's mind raced ahead of the car as they drove through traffic on their way to the store. She knew ShopTown had a big toy department. *The dolls are on third aisle, past the stuffed animals*, she reminded herself. *After that there's the remote-controlled cars, then the bicycles.*

As Jenny remembered the toys, she thought of something else she'd really like to buy. It was at the end of the last row. *I wish I could buy that flamingo night-light alarm clock. But I know it costs ten dollars. And I have only two dollars and fifty cents.*

At ShopTown, Jenny wandered up and down the aisles. *The tiny doll is only $2.49. I could buy that.* The detective note pad and spyglass were on the next aisle. *It cost $2.25. But I have a little notebook like that one. And I can use Mom's binoculars when I want to play spy.*

Before long, Jenny found herself at the end of the last row. She stared at the alarm clock with the flamingo on top. At the end of the flamingo's long neck, a light bulb was hidden in the bird's bill. But the price tag said $9.95.

I wish I had ten dollars, Jenny thought.

By the time her mother was ready to leave, Jenny still hadn't decided to buy anything. As she watched her mom pay at the checkout counter, she thought of something.

"Mom, I can't buy something that costs two dollars and fifty cents. What about the tax?" Jenny didn't understand all about taxes, but she knew you had to pay extra.

Mrs. Wallace nodded. "You're right. But when you're ready to buy something, I'll pay for the taxes. You spend your money on something you want."

"Thanks, Mom. When are we going shopping again?" While Jenny asked this question, she was looking at the rows of candy bars and gum. *I could spend my money on that,* she thought.

"We're going to the mall Saturday night," Mrs. Wallace answered. "You can shop again then, if you know what you want."

That night, Jenny and her mom read over her lesson.

"Abram thought that everything he owned had been given to him by God," Mrs. Wallace said.

Jenny thought about that. "God has given us a lot too, hasn't He?"

"Yes, He has," Mrs. Wallace agreed. "We have a home and all the things we need—and each other. But your lesson is about what we give back to God."

"What did Abram give back to God?" Jenny asked.

"One-tenth of everything he gained. Giving back one-tenth of what you earn is called giving a tithe."

Suddenly, Jenny sat up straight. "Does that mean I should give some of my two dollars and fifty cents to God?"

Mrs. Wallace nodded. "If you believe He helped you earn that money, then you should return a tenth of it to God. You would put twenty-five cents in a tithe envelope on the offering plate at church."

Jenny thought about that. "Then I would have only two dollars and twenty-five cents. I couldn't even buy that tiny doll. I couldn't buy anything but candy or gum."

Mrs. Wallace pushed her hair back. "I'm sure there are other things to buy. Or you could save the money."

I don't know if I really want to give my money to God, Jenny thought. *I need it!*

The next Sabbath in the Shoebox, Mrs. Shue talked about Abram again. "God gave Abram so many blessings he didn't really know what to do with them all."

"Wow, that would be like having too many toys to ever play with them all," Chris said. "I'd like that."

Mrs. Shue laughed. "It's more like having a partner or a teammate who's taking care of you."

Jenny raised her hand. "Mrs. Shue, why does God need our money?"

"He doesn't really need it, Jenny. The money we give for tithe helps pay for ministers and church work. But mostly, we need to give the money to remind ourselves that God really owns everything. Even us."

By the time she got to church, Jenny had decided what to do. She got a tithe envelope and wrote her name on it. On the tithe line, she wrote "25 cents." Then she dropped in two dimes and a nickel. When the deacons came by, she dropped the envelope in with a smile.

Inside, she was thinking, *I'm glad God is my partner and that He gives me so much. I'm happy to give a little part of my money back to Him.*

That night, she and her mom were on their way out the door when the phone rang. "Hello?" Mrs. Wallace answered. "Yes, Mrs. Miles. Just a moment." She put her hand over the phone. "Jenny, Mrs. Miles wants to speak to you."

Jenny took the phone. "Hello."

"Jenny, Mrs. Garrison told me how you helped her with her garage cleaning. I've decided to clean my garage too. Could I hire you to help me tomorrow?"

"I'd be happy to help you," Jenny answered. She was still smiling when she got in the car. "I'll be making more money," she told her mom. "Hey, maybe I can save it and buy the flamingo lamp after all."

Her mom just smiled.

Then Jenny remembered something else. "God is blessing me the same way He blessed Abram. Am I ever glad that He's my partner!"

QUESTIONS

1. Doesn't it feel good to earn money? What did you do to earn money this week?

2. Do you ever have a hard time deciding what to buy as Jenny did? Maybe you should save your money for something nice.

3. Paying tithe is giving part of God's money back to Him. Giving means you remember that you're His partner.

4. If you are partners with God, you can be sure He'll bless you—just as He blessed Abram.

11

STRANGERS FROM HEAVEN
DeeDee's Bright Idea

After the battle that rescued Lot, God spoke to Abram again. "You don't need to be afraid, Abram," God said. "I will always be here to protect you. And I will give you a great reward."

Abram sighed. "What reward would you give me, God? I have everything I could want except children. Now when I die, everything I have will be passed on to my servant and friend, Eliezer."

"No, Abram," God said. "You will have a son. Come outside, Abram. I want to show you something."

So Abram went outside. God said, "Look up at the sky. See all those stars? There are too many to even count. Someday, your family will be too big to count also."

Abram believed God. That's what made Abram God's friend—he had faith in whatever God said.

Even though Abram believed God, his wife Sarai didn't have as much faith. She said, "Abram, maybe God meant for us to have children a different way. I want you to marry my servant woman Hagar. Then when she has a child, we will raise it as our own."

So Abram did as Sarai asked. But it didn't work out very well. Sarai was even more unhappy than before. Hagar did have a son whom she named Ishmael. But he was not the son that God had promised Abram.

Thirteen years later, when Abram was ninety-nine years old, God came to him again. "Abram," God said, "you are going to be the father of a great family of people. So I am changing your name to Abraham. I am changing Sarai's name to Sarah because she is going to be the mother of a great nation of people."

Abram couldn't help laughing. "God, I am ninety-nine years old and Sarai is ninety. We are too old to have children."

"No," God said. "A year from now, you and Sarah are going to have a son. And you will name him Isaac."

Some time later, Abraham was resting in the shade of his tent during the hottest time of the day. He looked out and saw three men coming toward his tent. Abraham jumped up and ran to meet them. "Come and rest in the shade," he invited them. "Let me wash your feet and give you some food and drink before you continue on your way."

"Thank you," the travelers said. "We accept your kindness." So they stopped to rest under the shade of a tree while Abraham prepared their meal.

Abraham raced back to the tent. "Sarah, we have

guests. Please make some bread while I cook the meat."
When the food was ready, Abraham served the three men
and stood by while they ate.

"Where is your wife, Sarah?" one of the guests asked
Abraham.

"She's there in the tent," he answered.

The guest must have smiled. "When I visit again next
year, she will have a son."

Sarah was in the tent listening to their talk. When
she heard this, she laughed. She knew she was too old to
have a baby.

The guest said to Abraham, "Why did Sarah laugh?
She will have a baby. It doesn't matter how old she is.
Nothing is too hard for God."

Finally Abraham figured out who his visitors were—
it was God and two of His angels. When they left to
keep walking toward Sodom, Abraham walked with them.
God decided to tell Abraham why they were going to
Sodom.

"I hear that Sodom has become a very, very wicked
place," God said. "I'm going to see for myself. If the
people there are that evil, I will have to destroy the city."

The angels walked on toward Sodom while God
stopped to talk with His friend, Abraham. Abraham
couldn't help thinking about Lot and his family. He
asked, "Are you going to destroy the good people of
Sodom along with the bad ones? What if there are fifty
good people in Sodom?"

God said, "If there are fifty good people in Sodom, I
won't destroy it."

Abraham had another question. "What if there are only forty-five good people? Will you save the city for forty-five people?"

God said, "I will."

Abraham thought about Sodom. It was an evil place. "What if there are only thirty good people, God? Will you save the place for only thirty people?" The answer was yes.

Abraham asked about twenty people. God said, "I will save the city for twenty people."

Then Abraham asked one last question. "God, what if there are only ten people? Will you not destroy Sodom if there are only ten good people?"

"OK, Abraham," God said. "If only ten good people are there, the city will not be destroyed."

So Abraham went home. He was glad to worship a God he could talk to as a friend. He was very glad that he had been kind to strangers before he knew they were from heaven.

DeeDee's Bright Idea

Oh, Mother. Do I have to?"

DeeDee Adams was not happy. "I don't want to wear my winter dress," she muttered to herself. "It'll be too hot."

Mrs. Adams came to the door of DeeDee's room. "I know it's almost spring," she said, "but it's not warm enough to buy a spring dress yet. You'll either have to wear one of your old dresses or wear your winter dress again."

DeeDee whined, "But my old dresses are too small."

"When it's warm enough, we'll buy new dresses for spring and summer," her mom said. "But I can't afford to buy you a new dress that you'll only wear for a few weeks. Hurry, now, or we'll be late for Sabbath School."

DeeDee was quietly unhappy in the car. When they walked into the church, she noticed a family she hadn't seen before. *That girl has on a cool dress*, she thought. *And the little boys are wearing short-sleeve shirts. At least someone knows it's spring.*

"Good morning," Mrs. Adams said to the woman with the children. "Welcome to church. Can we help with anything?"

Before long, DeeDee was showing the girl, Marissa, to the Kindergarten room. Then she went on to the Shoebox.

"Our lesson is about Abraham," Mrs. Shue said. "When strangers walked toward his tents, he hurried to make them feel welcome. Why do you think he did that?"

"Because they were special visitors from heaven," Chris answered.

"Yes," Mrs. Shue agreed, "they were. But Abraham welcomed them before he knew who they were. Abraham welcomed all visitors that way. And he must have had many visitors, since he was a rich man by now. Why do you think he did that?"

"He wanted to make friends and not make enemies," Sammy guessed.

"He wanted to tell them about God," Jenny said.

Mrs. Shue nodded. "You may both be right. But the main reason why Abraham was kind to others is that it made him happy. He felt happy when he could help someone else."

DeeDee thought, *I'd be happy helping others too, if I was rich and I could buy all the things I wanted.*

In the car after church, DeeDee had a surprise. "I invited Marissa's family over for lunch," Mrs. Adams said. "Would you help me by finding the children something to play with while I'm getting lunch on the table?"

"Yes, Mother," DeeDee said grumpily. But she didn't really feel too grumpy. *It might be fun to play with Marissa,* she thought.

DeeDee got some of her old toys out for the little boys. Their eyes got as big as their smiles when she handed the toys to them. *Boy, you'd think they didn't have any toys,* she thought.

"Come on, I'll show you around," she told Marissa. "Let's go look at my room."

"Your dress sure is pretty," Marissa said. "I wish I had a pretty dress like that."

DeeDee's mouth fell open. "Th-thank you. I wish I had a nice spring dress like yours. My dress was too hot today." She looked at Marissa's dress again and realized that it was too small and a little faded. *Is that the only dress she has?* DeeDee wondered.

Later that afternoon, when the family was driving away, DeeDee turned to her mom. "Marissa and her family are poor, aren't they?"

Mrs. Adams nodded. "Marissa's mother is raising her

children alone. She works hard, but they don't have much except a little house on the edge of town."

"Can I give Marissa some of my old dresses?" DeeDee blurted out the question.

Her mother looked at her. "This sounds like a different girl than the one getting dressed this morning."

"Well," DeeDee mumbled, "I didn't know I had so many."

"We'll pack some things in a box and drop them by their house tomorrow," Mrs. Adams decided.

The next day when they stopped in front of the tiny little house, DeeDee almost felt like crying. Mr. Adams waited in the car while DeeDee and her mother walked up the cracked sidewalk and stood by the weed-filled flowerbed. Mrs. Adams knocked, but no one answered.

"Oh, that's right," Mrs. Adams remembered. "She told me that she had to work today. The children are at the babysitter's. I guess we'll just leave our box here on the porch."

DeeDee turned and stared at the yard. She thought about her own yard, with its bright new flowers. "There's a swing set," she said, pointing at a rusty set of bars, "but the swings are broken and the slide fell off."

Suddenly, she couldn't stand it. "Mother! Let's do something about this."

"What? Do what?"

DeeDee talked fast. "Couldn't we get some of those flowers like the ones you planted in our yard and plant them here?"

"DeeDee, that would be a lot of work. We'd have to clean out these flowerbeds first. I don't know, we'd have to see what your father thinks."

"Daddy," DeeDee called as she ran to the car, "can we fix up their yard and surprise them? You know, plant flowers and maybe fix the swings?"

Mr. Adams looked around. "DeeDee, it's very nice of you to want to do this for them. I think I could help a little."

Before long, they were back from the store. DeeDee was digging up the flowerbed with a little shovel. Her mother was right behind her planting beautiful flowers. Her dad was putting new chains on the swings and bolting the slide back into place.

Finally, with all the tools back in the car, they stopped to look around. "It's beautiful," Mother said. "DeeDee, that was a great idea." Mr. Adams wrapped them both in a hug.

Before they could drive away, Marissa and her family pulled up into the driveway. Just seeing their faces as they stared out the car windows made DeeDee decide something.

Abraham was right, she thought. *The best reason to be kind to others is how it makes you feel.*

DeeDee felt happy all over.

QUESTIONS

1. Do you ever wake up feeling grumpy as DeeDee did?

2. Aren't you glad when spring comes?

3. How would you like to have angels visit you as Abraham did? Would you treat them better than you would treat other people? Why?

4. DeeDee learned that being kind to others made her happy. What have you done to make yourself happy?

12
CHAPTER

SAVED FROM SODOM
Flash Flood!

The two angels who ate at Abraham's tent traveled on to Sodom and arrived at the city gates just before dark. Lot was there, and when he saw the two strangers, he ran to meet them. He knew how dangerous and evil the city of Sodom was. "Please come to my house and stay for the evening," he asked the strangers.

"No, no," they said. "We'll just stay in the city park."

Lot begged them. "No! You must come to my house. It's not safe for you to stay outside after dark."

Finally, the strangers agreed and went to Lot's house for supper and for the night. When it was nearly time for bed, Lot heard shouting outside his door. When he looked out, he knew that a crowd had come to take his visitors.

"Bring the strangers to us," the crowd shouted.

Lot slipped out the door to talk to the crowd. "Please, go away and leave these men alone." But the people in the crowd just got angrier. They started to attack Lot.

Suddenly, the door flew open and the two strangers dragged Lot back inside. But before they closed the door, everyone in the crowd had been struck blind.

Now Lot knew that his visitors were angels. "We are going to destroy this city," they told Lot. "But you and your family can escape. You must all leave tonight."

Two of Lot's daughters lived at home, but the others were married. Lot spent most of the night trying to convince them to leave the city. They just laughed at him. Finally, when it was nearly dawn, the angels told Lot to escape with his wife and two daughters. "Hurry," they said, "you're running out of time!"

But Lot just couldn't hurry and leave everything and everyone behind. The angels took him and his family by the hands and pulled them to the city gates. "Now run for your lives!" they said. "Don't look back or stop anywhere in the valley. Don't stop until you reach the mountains!"

"Oh, please," Lot sobbed, "I can't make it to the mountains. Can I run to Zoar and be safe? It's just a little town."

"OK," the angel said. "I won't destroy that town. But hurry! I can't destroy Sodom until you are safe inside."

Lot and his daughters ran as fast as they could to Zoar. But Lot's wife started thinking about all the things she liked about Sodom. She stopped and looked back—and she turned into a pillar of salt.

As soon as the rest of the family was safe, fire rained down on Sodom and all the cities of the Jordan River valley. Everything in the whole valley was destroyed.

When Abraham saw the smoke coming up from the valley, he knew that Sodom had been destroyed. God had not been able to save the city, but He sent His angels to save everyone who would leave the wicked city behind.

Flash Flood!

*S*wish, *swish, swish, swish.*

Sammy Tan watched the windshield wipers go back and forth as the car crawled down the road. "Grandfather, how much farther is it?" he asked.

Grandfather Tan strained to see through the heavy rain. "I'm not sure, Sammy. The Websters live on River Road. If it weren't raining so hard, we would be there by now. I hope I haven't missed the turn to River Road. They're expecting us before lunch."

Sammy sighed and sat back in his seat. He liked going out to the Websters' farm. But it always took too long to get there.

From his place next to Sammy, Angel 44 received a message from heaven. "The rain will cause the river to flood. Begin the special protection plan."

Angel 36 whispered in Grandmother Tan's ear, "Turn on the radio."

"Let's turn on the radio," Grandmother Tan said. "Maybe some music will help the time go faster." She clicked the knob, and for a few minutes, quiet music filled the car. Then a voice interrupted.

"The National Weather Service has issued a Flash Flood

Warning for the river area. After last night's rain, the river was filled to the top of its banks. Rain this morning is causing flooding in the river valleys."

Angel 19 whispered to Grandfather Tan, "Slow down."

Grandfather slowed down the car. "Maybe we should go back. We're very close to the river."

"Will the flood come here?" Sammy asked. He wiped a circle on his window and tried to see out.

Angel 44 received another message. "The floodwater is headed your way. Let's move those people out."

Sammy pointed to the window. "Grandfather, the water is all the way up to the edge of the road."

"We're going back," Grandfather Tan decided. He turned the car around carefully.

"Are we going to be OK?" Sammy said in a whisper.

Grandmother Tan reached back and patted his leg. "Sammy, we pray every day for God's angels to be with us and protect us. I'm sure they are with us now."

Angel 44 scooted closer to Sammy.

They moved slowly down the road in the heavy rain. To Sammy, it looked as though someone was pouring buckets of water over the car. "Can you see anything, Grandfather?" he asked.

Grandfather Tan shook his head. "Not very much. I wish the window defogger would work better."

Angel 19 waved a hand over the windshield.

"Now it's working," Grandfather Tan said. Everyone leaned forward to see better.

"Look!" Grandmother Tan pointed forward. "The road is covered with water."

Flash Flood!

Grandfather stopped the car. Sammy got worried again. "Shouldn't we keep going before it gets even deeper?"

"No, Sammy," Grandmother Tan answered. "You should never drive in flood water. We can't be sure how deep it is. And moving water can float a car away before the people inside can get out."

"I'm going to step out and look around," Grandfather Tan decided. "Maybe the rain will let up just a little and I can figure out which way to go." He opened his door and stepped out. Big raindrops hit Sammy before the door slammed shut.

"Grandmother, let's pray, OK?"

"OK, Sammy." Grandmother Tan closed her eyes.

"Jesus, please keep us safe in this flood," Sammy prayed. "Help Grandfather know what to do. Amen."

Angel 19 spread his wings over the car. For a moment, the rain slowed down.

The car door popped open and rain flew in again. "Well," Grandfather Tan said, "grab your jackets and things. We're heading out."

"Are you sure?" Grandmother Tan asked.

"The water is rising fast," Grandfather Tan answered. "It's behind us and in front of us. There's a barn up ahead. We'll head for that."

When Sammy pushed his door open, the rain pounded on his head. He stepped out, raised his jacket over his head with one hand, and reached for Grandmother Tan with his other hand. "Let's stay close together," she called.

The water was rushing around Sammy's feet before

they had gone five steps. "It's cold!" he shouted as the water washed over his sneakers.

"Watch your step," Grandfather Tan called.

Angel 44 stepped along with Sammy. His hands kept Sammy's shoes from slipping on the slimy mud.

The water got all the way up to Sammy's knees before they got past the deepest part. They splashed through the last puddles and rushed in through the open doors. "It sure feels good to get out of the rain," Sammy said.

"Go over to that ladder," Grandfather Tan called from the doorway. "The water could be here any minute. By the time Sammy had climbed up to the loft, the water was starting to flow in like a stream.

Angel 44 contacted Control. "The water's rising fast. We need help here."

The answer came back. "Just help them hold on for a few more minutes."

"What's Grandfather doing?" Sammy called down to his grandmother, who was standing at the bottom of the ladder.

"He thinks he heard something outside," she answered, "so he's going to look out the door. He'll be right back."

Suddenly, Sammy thought he heard something too. "Was that another car?" he asked. Then a big roar answered his question.

Mr. Webster's big farm truck rolled right in through the big, open doors. He stuck his head out the window. "I thought you folks were coming to my house, not my barn," he called out with a big grin.

Sammy scrambled down and crowded onto Grandfather Tan's lap in the truck. They backed out carefully and drove away from the main road. "You almost made it to River Road. The water hasn't risen high enough to cover it yet."

"What were you doing out driving around in a flood?" Sammy asked.

"Well, for some reason I got to thinking about you guys," Mr. Webster said. "I drove down to the main road to see how high the water was, and there was your car, floating along. I figured you'd head for the barn, and there you were."

"I'm sure glad you found us," Sammy said.

Angel 44 relaxed. "It was a good plan," he reported, "and it worked perfectly. Thanks for your help, everyone."

The next week in the Shoebox, Mrs. Shue said, "God sent angels to protect Lot. Does He protect us today?"

Angel 44 laughed when Sammy's hand went up first.

QUESTIONS

1. Have you ever been in a flood? What did you do to stay safe?

2. Did you know that God sends a special angel to be with you all the time? Your angel never leaves you.

3. It's important to pray and ask God to be with you every day. Did you remember to pray today?

4. God watches us and protects us when something scary happens—as He did for Lot. Aren't you glad?

CHAPTER 13

ABRAHAM'S TEST
Willie's Baseball Treasure

The next year, just as God promised, Abraham and Sarah had a baby boy. They named him Isaac, just as God had planned. It was a very happy time for them, but there was a problem. Abraham's other son, Ishmael, and his mother were not happy to see the new baby.

Sarah wanted to send them away, but Abraham wasn't sure. He loved his son Ishmael. He prayed and asked God. God said, "Go ahead and send them away. I will take care of Ishmael and his mother. I will make a great nation of people from Ishmael too." So Abraham sent Ishmael and his mother away to find a new home.

Years went by, and God decided to test Abraham's faith again. When Isaac was about twenty years old, He said, "Abraham, take your son—your only son, Isaac—and go to the land called Moriah. There I want you to build an altar and offer Isaac as a sacrifice to Me on a mountain I will show you."

Abraham must have been shocked and scared. How

could God ask him to kill his own son? But Abraham knew God's voice, and he had learned to trust God. So he went and woke up Isaac.

"Wake up, son," he said. "God wants us to travel to Moriah and offer a sacrifice on a mountain there."

Isaac didn't argue with his father. He had gone with Abraham to offer sacrifices many times. He helped load wood onto the donkey and gather the things they needed for the trip. Then he and his father and two servants left to go to Moriah.

They traveled for two days, and on the third day Abraham saw the mountain God wanted them to go to. "Stay here," he told the servants. "Isaac and I will go up the mountain and offer the sacrifice."

So Isaac carried the wood and Abraham carried the knife and the fire. As they climbed the mountain trail, Isaac had a question. "Father, we have the fire and the wood for a sacrifice. But where is the lamb?"

Abraham had to clear his throat and wipe his eyes before he could answer. "God will give us a lamb to sacrifice, son," he finally said.

When they reached the right spot, Abraham and Isaac built the altar. They stacked the stones and placed the wood on top. Then Abraham had to explain what God had told him to do.

Isaac was bigger and stronger than his father. He knew that he could run away or even pick his father up and carry him down the mountain to home. But he didn't. He trusted his father. And he had learned to trust God the same way his father did. So Isaac let his father tie his hands and feet, just as they had tied many lambs before, and lay him down on the altar.

Abraham didn't want to sacrifice Isaac. He didn't understand why it should happen. But he had learned to trust God before, so he trusted Him now. He raised the knife with one hand and then . . .

"Abraham! Abraham!" a voice called. It was God's angel. "Don't hurt your son. I know now that you trust God—even with your only son's life."

Abraham didn't waste a second cutting the strings that tied Isaac's hand and hugging him right down from the altar. Then he saw a male sheep whose horns were caught in a bush. "There's our sacrifice," he told Isaac. They caught the sheep and sacrificed it on the altar.

Abraham had passed the test. And so had Isaac. Now God was ready to make their family a great nation.

Willie's Baseball Treasure

Hey, Willie, are you going to the Super Sports Show this weekend?"

Willie Teller was playing catch with his friend Chris. He tossed the baseball to Chris's glove and asked, "What sports show?"

"It's a sports collector's show," Chris answered. He caught the ball and tossed a low one. "You know, where people buy and sell rare or famous sports things."

Willie caught it on the first bounce and threw it high up in the air towards Chris. "That's right, I remember now. Before he left town yesterday, my dad said we might take his baseball to show. He has a ball signed by Joe Gerardo. He's going to give it to me one of these days."

Chris froze. The ball hit his glove and bounced out. "What? Did you say it was signed by Joe Gerardo? He was one of the best players ever. That's a real treasure. It must be worth a lot of money!"

Willie smiled big. Later, at home, he saw the red telephone answering machine light blinking. He pushed the button and listened as his dad's voice spoke.

"Willie, listen carefully because this is important. I need you to do something for me. The next time you and your mom go to town, get my baseball—you know, the one on the shelf in my room—and take it to Shorty's Sport Shop. Give it to Shorty behind the counter and tell him it's from me. Thanks. I'll be home soon!"

I wonder why he wants me to do that, Willie thought. He took the ball off the shelf and looked at Joe Gerardo's signature. *I hope Dad hasn't forgotten his promise to give it to me someday.*

"Mom, why does Dad want me to take this ball to that store?" Willie asked on the way there.

"I don't know," she answered. "He didn't tell me. But I need to go to the flower shop next door, so I'll just let you go in and drop the ball off."

Willie rolled in and stared at the posters and pennants on the walls. *Wow,* he thought, *this place has stuff about football, basketball, baseball, everything!*

He got in line in front of the cash register and listened to the people in front of him. "What have you got there?" the short man behind the counter asked a teenager.

That must be Shorty, Willie thought.

"These baseball cards," the kid answered. "How much are they worth?"

Shorty looked them over carefully. Then he said, "I'll give you one dollar for each one." He handed over the money, and the kid walked away. A man showed Shorty a signed photograph of a football player. "I'll give you ten dollars," Shorty said.

Willie was next, but he backed away. *Shorty buys sports things from people,* he said to himself. *Dad didn't want me to sell the ball, did he?*

As he rolled down the aisle, Willie argued with himself. *Dad wouldn't sell this ball. He promised it to me. But Dad did say to bring it here and give it to Shorty. Why would he do that?*

Willie tried to think of reasons why. *Maybe Dad doesn't know how much money it's worth. Or maybe he really needs the money for something.* That made him feel a little scared. *Maybe Dad doesn't really want me to have the treasure.* That made him feel sad.

Maybe Dad doesn't think I would take care of it. He almost felt angry at that idea. He rolled back toward the counter.

"Sure," he heard Shorty say, "we buy and sell almost anything."

Willie rolled right past him and out the door.

"Hey," his mom said, "I thought you were going to leave the ball at the store."

"I just couldn't, Mom," Willie said. "It's worth a lot of money. I can't just give it to Shorty."

Mrs. Teller nodded slowly. "But I heard your dad's message too. He said to bring it here and give it to Shorty. He must have had a good reason for it."

"Are you sure?" Willie asked.

"He's your father, Willie. What do you think?"

Willie turned and rolled slowly back into the store. *I guess Dad knows what he's doing—I sure don't! But it's what he said to do, so he must have a reason.*

"My name is Willie Teller," Willie said to Shorty. "My dad said to give this to you." He held up the ball.

"Teller," Shorty mumbled. "Oh yes. Your dad's baseball." He took the ball and examined it closely. "It's beautiful. Here, give this envelope to your dad."

With that, Shorty took the ball away, and Willie rolled sadly out to the car. His mind was whirling with questions, but he didn't say a word all the way home.

That Sabbath in the Shoebox, Mrs. Shue talked about Abraham. "Abraham trusted God's voice, even when that voice told him to sacrifice Isaac. Abraham didn't want to do it, but he was willing to give up what he valued most—his son—because he believed that God knew best."

I know a little about how that feels, Willie thought as he listened.

DeeDee asked, "Mrs. Shue, why did Abraham trust God?"

Mrs. Shue smiled. "Abraham knew God well enough to believe that God had a good plan, whatever it was. He chose to trust in God."

Maybe I should do that about Dad's ball, Willie thought. In just a flash, he made up his mind. Then he closed his eyes. *God,* Willie prayed, *help me to trust Dad about his baseball. And to trust you the way Abraham did. Amen.*

For some reason, Willie felt pretty good. By the time they picked up Mr. Teller at the airport that night, Willie had almost forgotten about the ball. It seemed that his dad had forgotten too, because no one mentioned the ball at all.

"Willie, are you ready to go?" Mr. Teller called from the kitchen the next day.

"Go where?" Willie asked.

"To the Super Sports Show," Mr. Teller said. "Where did you put the envelope Shorty gave you? It has our tickets."

Willie handed it over without any questions. Once they got to the show, he forgot about the baseball and enjoyed looking at all the exhibits with his dad. Then a voice called out to them.

"Hey, Teller! Over here." It was Shorty. Willie felt his heart sink. Mr. Teller got a big smile on his face.

"Shorty, did you get the ball?" Mr. Teller asked. Shorty nodded and stepped aside so they could see.

There, inside a clear glass globe, was the ball. A gold plaque underneath it said, "Signed by Joe Gerardo."

Willie almost didn't notice that. He was busy staring at the sign on the wall behind it. That sign said, "Owned by Willie Teller. Not for sale."

"You weren't worried about the ball, were you?" Mr. Teller asked. "I wanted to surprise you, so I'm glad you did just what I told you to. Do you like it?" He knelt down beside his son. Willie answered him with a hug.

ABRAHAM'S TEST

"It's my favorite treasure," Willie said. "And I wasn't worried—not after I decided to trust you."

QUESTIONS
1. Do you collect anything? Baseball cards, rocks, or feathers?
2. Why didn't Willie want to give the ball to Shorty?
3. Think of a time when you had to trust an adult (such as going to the doctor or waiting for your mom or dad). How did you feel?
4. Why did you choose to trust them?
5. Why can you trust God, even when you aren't sure what's happening?

If you enjoyed this book, you'll enjoy these other Shoebox Kids adventures:

Book 1 - *The Case of the Secret Code*
    Topic: Prayer. 0-8163-1249-4
Book 2 - *The Mysterious Treasure Map*
    Topic: Baptism. 0-8163-1256-7
Book 3 - *Jenny's Cat-napped Cat*
    Topic: Forgiveness. 0-8163-1277-X
Book 4 - *The Missing Combination Mystery*
    Topic: Jealousy. 0-8163-1276-1
Book 5 - *The Broken Dozen Mystery*
    Topic: Helping others. 0-8163-1332-6
Book 6 - *The Wedding Dress Disaster*
    Topic: Commitment. 0-8163-1355-5
Book 7 - *The Clue in the Secret Passage*
    Topic: Bible. 0-8163-1386-5
Book 8 - *The Rockslide Rescue*
    Topic: Trust in God. 0-8163-1387-3
Book 9 - *The Secret of the Hidden Room*
    Topic: Prejudice. 0-8163-1682-1
Book 10 - *Adventure on Wild Horse Mountain*
    Topic: Judging Others. 0-8163-1683-X
Book 11 - *Rattlesnake River Adventure*
    Topic: Holding grudges/forgiveness. 0-8163-1757-7

$6.99US/$10.49Cdn

Order from your ABC by calling **1-800-765-6955**, or get online and shop our virtual store at
<www.adventistbookcenter.com>.
    •Read a chapter from your favorite book
    •Order online
    •Sign up for email notices on new products

Animal Stories
...e Whole Family Can Enjoy!

...rted with a perfectly pesky pet parrot named Julius ... pal Mitch. Then came a rascally red fox, a wildly ...raccoon, a curiously comical cow, and a thunder cat by ...me of Thor! But all of them help kids celebrate God's ...on with laughter and wonder. Collect the entire "herd" ...get a belly laugh or two yourself from the **Julius &** **...ends** series.

...perback. US$6.99, Can$10.49 each.

Book 1 - *Julius, the Perfectly Pesky Pet Parrot*. 0-8163-1173-0
Book 2 - *Julius Again!* 0-8163-1239-7
Book 3 - *Tina, the Really Rascally Red Fox*. 0-8163-1321-0
Book 4 - *Skeeter, the Wildly Wacky Raccoon*. 0-8163-1388-1
Book 5 - *Lucy, the Curiously Comical Cow*. 0-8163-1582-5
Book 6 - *Thor, the Thunder Cat*. 0-8163-1703-8

Available at your local ABC. Call 1-800-765-6955 to order.